GLASGOW

in the age of the tram

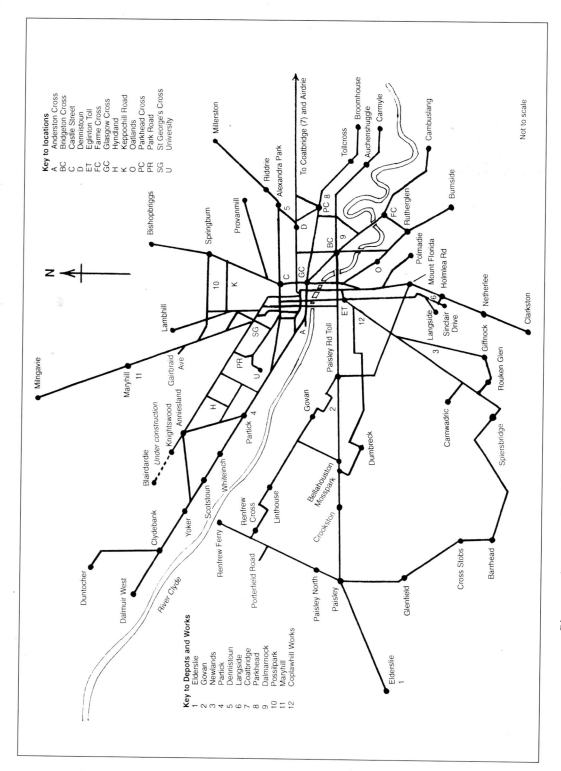

Key to locations

A	Anderston Cross
BC	Bridgeton Cross
C	Castle Street
D	Dennistoun
ET	Eglinton Toll
FC	Farme Cross
GC	Glasgow Cross
H	Hyndland
K	Keppochill Road
O	Oatlands
PC	Parkhead Cross
PR	Park Road
SG	St George's Cross
U	University

Key to Depots and Works

1	Elderslie
2	Govan
3	Newlands
4	Partick
5	Dennistoun
6	Langside
7	Coatbridge
8	Parkhead
9	Dalmarnock
10	Possilpark
11	Maryhill
12	Coplawhill Works

To Coatbridge (7) and Airdrie

Not to scale

Diagrammatic representation of Glasgow Corporation tramways in passenger service as at 1 January 1949.

GLASGOW

in the age of the tram
1950-62

Brian Patton

· THE NOSTALGIA OF BRITAIN ·
from
The NOSTALGIA *Collection*

First published in 1994 as *Another Nostalgic Look at Glasgow Trams Since 1950*
Republished in this format 2005

British Library Cataloguing in Publication Data

A catalogue record for this book is available from the British Library.

ISBN 1 85794 247 7

Silver Link Publishing Ltd
The Trundle
Ringstead Road
Great Addington
Kettering
Northants NN14 4BW

Tel/Fax: 01536 330588
email: sales@nostalgiacollection.com
Website:
www.nostalgiacollection.com

Printed and bound in Great Britain

SLP

A Silver Link book
from
The NOSTALGIA *Collection*

There must be at least eight trams visible in this view of Renfield Street at West George Street, taken at the end of the morning peak on 13 March 1959 – and never a bus in sight! Car 24 on service 25 leads the procession, with a Mk 2 Ford Zephyr parked outside the bank.

CONTENTS

BIBLIOGRAPHY

Cormack, Ian L. *Glasgow Trams beyond the
Boundary*
Green Goddesses Go East
Cowan, James *From Glasgow's Treasure Chest*
Fitzpayne, E. R. L. *A Report on the Future
Development of Passenger Transport in
Glasgow*
Stewart, Ian *The Glasgow Tramcar*
Thomson, D. L. *A Handbook of Glasgow
Tramways*
Worsdall, Frank *The Tenement – A Way of
Life*
The City that Disappeared

Young, A. M. and Doak, A. M. *Glasgow at a
Glance*

Periodicals
Modern Tramway, 1945 onwards
Scottish Tramlines/Scottish Transport, 1963
onwards

There are numerous other books on the trams
and transport of Glasgow, and literally
hundreds on the city itself; those mentioned
above have been particularly useful for
reference in the production of this book.

ACKNOWLEDGEMENTS

Although more than 40 years have now elapsed since the last run of a tramcar in normal service in Glasgow, interest in the cars is as strong as ever, as was amply demonstrated by the demand for Silver Link Publishing's original *A Nostalgic Look at...* volumes on the city's trams.

Most of the photographs included here were taken by myself, during school holidays or after classes at University. The older views were taken with a very simple folding Brownie. It cost 3s 3½d to have a film developed and printed, not leaving much change out of 5 shillings pocket money per week! In the late 1950s I used an Ensign Epsilon and, for the last two years, a Kodak 35mm Retinette, which is still giving yeoman service. Many pictures were taken on dull or wet days and I make no apology for the inclusion of such views; that is how it was, and that is how many people best remember the Glasgow tram. There were of course good years, and the summer of 1959 was especially fine, but the vision of a Coronation, with its cosy saloons and attractive lighting, bearing down out of the wet darkness is one that has tended to stick in the mind!

I have not attempted in this book to provide either a general history or a technical treatise. The former remains to be written, while readers who require the latter are referred to Ian Stewart's classic study *The Glasgow Tram*.

Instead, I have concentrated on the period from 1945 to the end, in an attempt to explain the factors that led to the abandonment.

We did not know then the magnitude of the changes that were about to come upon the city, far beyond the demise of the trams, and readers who know the city may judge for themselves how far Glasgow has actually progressed since 1962. Possibly the most encouraging feature is that the city has learned its lesson, and vandalism such as that which ruined Charing Cross in the interests of motorway construction is unlikely to be repeated!

I am grateful to those who have helped by lending their own photographs to expand the range of the book, in particular Willie Guthrie of East Kilbride, who so generously allowed me access to his collection. Ellen and the staff at the Photo Centre in Berwick have done a grand job with the reproduction of the older photographs; the staff of the Glasgow Room in the Mitchell Library have been most helpful in tracing material for captions; and Martin Jenkins of Online Video and Richard Wiseman, Editor of *Tramway Review*, also deserve my thanks for their help. Finally I owe a considerable debt to Mrs I. MacLachlan for her abiding interest and encouragement, and to Bob who has for too long had to put up with a house full of tram photographs and a garden full of weeds!

INTRODUCTION: THE DECLINE OF THE GLASGOW TRAM

Shortly before the end of the Second World War, as city authorities turned to the task of creating a brave new post-war world, an exhibition of town planning was held in the Glasgow Art Gallery. It featured among other displays a model of the tramway of the future; this had a central reservation in the middle of the road, as already used in Great Western Road, but with the difference that this tramway emerged from a tunnel. It ran between houses of a very pre-war style and the ornate poles that supported the overhead wire were of a distinctly Victorian appearance, but the single-deck tram bore more than a passing resemblance to the North American PCC car, at that time the world's most up-to-date design of tram. In one sense it was even more modern, since it was fitted with Glasgow's normal bow collector, in place of the trolley pole used on PCC cars. The message was clear – the trams would have an assured part to play in the development of the new post-war city. With a new and energetic manager, Mr E. R. L. Fitzpayne, who had assumed office in 1943, it was certain that there would be some interesting developments in store. That these would include trams was confirmed by Mr Fitzpayne in an address to the Royal Philosophical Society of Glasgow in February 1944.

The first planning report of the post-war period was one made by the City Engineer Robert Bruce in 1945. With the idealism typical of the time, he proposed a three-tier transport system, one tier of which was to be light rail lines worked by 'electric vehicles'; these would serve various areas in the south and converge on a subway beneath Queen Street in the centre before branching out along the median strips of new motorways to serve Easterhouse in the east and Knightswood in the west. Buses would act as feeders to the new lines. As with so many of the plans published in the first flush of post-war enthusiasm, little came of the Bruce Report.

While the transport system was certainly somewhat run-down by comparison with its condition in 1939, it had not reached the state of decrepitude of many English tramways, since the sheer necessity of coping with wartime traffic had made it essential to continue with a reasonable standard of maintenance. Nor had the tramways been greatly affected by bombing. It did not take very long before the permanent way gangs and the works staff had caught up with arrears of maintenance, and during 1946 and 1947 many freshly overhauled cars were to be seen on the streets. Meanwhile, in Coplawhill Works a new tramcar was taking shape, and when 1005 appeared in December 1947 the citizens of Glasgow realised that the promises made in 1944 had not been empty and that the Transport Department was once again intent on putting Glasgow at the forefront of development.

Unlike the tram of the exhibition, this was a double-decker, but it was of single-ended design, unlike the rest of the Glasgow fleet and the trams of every other British system save Rotherham. It was superbly comfortable since it was slightly wider than the rest of the fleet and the seats were not reversible. The high standard of lighting already reached in the Coronation trams was amply surpassed by that in the new one, whose fluorescent tubes shed light of a clarity not before achieved in any public service vehicle at a time when many city streets and not a few homes were still bathed in the yellow glare of incandescent gas. In fact, there were even complaints about the brightness of the lighting! By day the eye-catching livery of three shades of blue commanded attention wherever the car went, while at night the lighting had much the same effect. It was one of the most handsome trams ever to run in Britain.

However, the experiment with 1005 also showed up many of the defects that were to plague all attempts to develop a modern tramway system in Glasgow. Since it had a unique control system, it could be driven only by crews specially trained for it. Moreover, passengers at first boarded at the front and alighted at the rear, and while this arrangement would pose no problems in the 1990s, it did in 1947, and time was wasted at stops while would-be riders ran from the rear to the front. It was even more confusing for motorists when passengers suddenly emerged from the rear door, and there were some very near misses. In the end, the Department gave up trying to change the habits of several lifetimes and in 1949 altered the passenger flow to allow boarding at the rear.

Nor were any alterations made to the layout of the tracks to cope with a single-ended tram, as was then being done in many European cities, and 1005 could only operate on a few services, mainly the 33 circle round Springburn and short workings on the 18. Gradually the car's non-standard features were eliminated until it was finally rebuilt as a slightly odd – the two ends were not quite the same – double-ended car, with ancient seats from a scrapped Standard. It was a brave experiment, not fully followed through, and in that way it typified much of the post-war history of the trams. Ironically, had it survived in its original form and had the trams lasted into the era of one-person operation, it would have been an ideal prototype for that system.

A new fleet of trams appeared from 1948 to 1952, when 100 Cunarders took to the streets of the city. These were fast and comfortable (once they had been cured of their initial tendency to roll), but much less innovative than 1005. The proposed single-decker of 1944 never did get built, though the model continued to appear at events such as the annual 'Modern Homes' exhibition. Later, in 1949, the General Manager suggested that ten of the Cunarders should be constructed as 44-seat single-deckers, with a central entrance, but the Transport Committee was unable to come to a decision about this and the design ultimately appeared in Leeds in the form of 601 and 602 of 1953, after A. B. Findlay had gone from Glasgow to become manager in that city. For the last six trams to be built for Glasgow, in 1954, the Department reverted to the design of the Coronation trams of 1937, perhaps the favourite of the public.

While these developments were going ahead in the tram fleet, a Fifty Year Plan for the development of the city was published, and Mr Fitzpayne, as part of this, produced in 1948 a report on the future development of transport facilities. For its time this document was incredibly far-seeing, and in the 21st century it still reads as an example of modern thinking, anticipating many of the ideas that are now put into practice as light rapid transit develops in Britain and elsewhere. Briefly, it proposed the electrification of certain suburban railway lines, the reconstruction to standard gauge of certain tramway lines (Glasgow used a gauge of 4ft 7¾in), and the construction of subways in the city centre. The railway and tramway lines were to be operated as one unit, with much use being made of railway formations for the light rapid transit system, as has been done with Metrolink in Manchester. There would also be running in the median strip of motorways, and a new subway would link lines north and south of the Clyde. Stations would be not less than half a mile apart and would be unstaffed, and platforms would be enclosed by partitions with sliding doors that would correspond with those on the cars, as on the modern French VAL system. It was planned to use third rail current collection, mainly to ease maintenance in the tunnels.

The vehicles to be used were single-deck two-car units that would be coupled in pairs when necessary. There was a touch of the Cunarder trams about the design, although the double doors, of which there were to be two sets on each side of each car, had half-moon windows of an aspect very typical of the 1930s. Like the Cunarders, the light rail vehicles would have had electro-pneumatic control and air brakes. The cars were of course to be single-deckers, 45 feet long and 9 feet wide, with seats for 47 passengers each and a very moderate standing capacity of 30. The seats themselves were to be of twin-tub type and would all face the direction of travel, being turned at termini by compressed air. With stations spaced half a mile apart, the cars would have an average speed of 25.6mph. Apart from the gimmick of the reversible seats, the cars would have looked rather like the Stadtbahn cars supplied to Stuttgart in the last decade and were far ahead of contemporary practice.

The use of third rail collection, which would have made street running impossible, would have been a drawback, but otherwise these ideas are very similar to those put into practice in cities such as Manchester and Karlsruhe and formed part of more recent planning for light rapid transit in Glasgow. The actual tram services to be converted in this way included the line along Great Western Road to Drumchapel, a line that appeared also in later plans. Some other tram services were to be converted to bus or trolleybus operation. Unfortunately no action was taken on these far-sighted plans, which, had they been implemented, could not only have spared Glasgow's transport 50 years of decline, but also put the city back to the position it had once occupied as a world leader in urban transport.

Meanwhile there was both contraction and expansion in services. In 1948 a dispute had arisen with Lanarkshire County Council about rate payments for the track on the Uddingston route, a considerable portion of which lay outside the city boundary. As it proved impossible to reach any agreement, the tram service, No 29, was curtailed at Broomhouse from 29 August 1948 and replaced by a bus service, running into the city by a different route and at a higher fare of 5d instead of the tram's 4d. Again this re-arrangement showed many of the aspects of muddled thinking that was to characterise the last decade of the trams. There were already plenty of buses running to Uddingston, not to mention two railway services, and presumably most of the tram passengers had chosen that form of transport in preference to a bus and were unlikely to make a point of travelling by a GCT rather than a Central SMT bus. More importantly, the new bus service ran to the city via Carmyle and London Road, thus breaking an established travel pattern. The new terminus served only a crematorium and the Glasgow zoo, and there was very little traffic. Most trams on the 29 turned back at Tollcross.

Elsewhere in the city the trams were under attack from a different source. Several members of the Corporation had conceived a great interest in the trolleybus and in 1945 it had been agreed that tram service 2, from Provanmill to Polmadie via High Street, should be converted to this form of transport as an experiment. In itself this would not have mattered greatly, had not the Ministry of Transport frowned on the parallel operation of trolleybuses and trams fitted with bow collectors, thus necessitating the withdrawal of service 19, which also ran via High Street, and its replacement by motor buses. It was also decided to construct a branch line to Oatlands, and in turn this forced the withdrawal of service 10 between Glasgow Cross and Rutherglen. The end result, when the trolleybuses finally entered service in April 1949, was that another traffic pattern was disrupted, with large numbers of passengers transferring to the Central SMT buses. Much the same happened four years later, when in 1953 the trams to Clarkston were replaced by trolleybuses and the through service to Victoria Road was broken. All these developments harmed the trams without helping the newly established trolleybuses to find favour with the public.

A further abandonment had taken place in December 1949 when the local service running up Kilbowie Road from Clydebank to Duntocher, worked exclusively by single-deck cars, was replaced by single-deck buses.

However, it was not all gloom in the immediate post-war years. A new branch was constructed to Carnwadric and opened for traffic on 7 November 1948. Initially worked as service 14B, it was soon renumbered 31, then in August 1949 became part of the 25. This branch was only about 600 yards in length and was on conventional street track. The other post-war extension, from Knightswood Cross to Blairdardie, opened on 31 July 1949, was laid out on spacious reserved track, marked off by grass verges and with centre poles for the overhead, and was an example of all that was modern in tramway practice. The line was to have continued further to Drumchapel or Duntocher, but there was a problem with the bridge over the Forth & Clyde Canal immediately to the west of the new terminus. While it would have been possible to have fitted tramway overhead to an opening bridge (as is done in Amsterdam and was done in Leith), there were already plans to close the Canal to navigation and Glasgow was unwilling to spend money on such a bridge when it might be used for only a few years. So the trams stopped at Blairdardie, and in fact the Canal outlived them by a short time.

There were also various cases of alteration to existing services to provide improved facilities. For example, the short working on service 1 terminating at Scotstounhill was extended to Scotstoun West on 19 May 1947, while service 4 was extended in Springburn in 1951. There were also several attempts to establish circular services in the eastern part of the city, which saw at various dates between 1946 and 1953 the operation of services 34, 35 and 36, none of which seemed to attract enough custom to become permanent. Curiously, while there was also a 40, Glasgow did not operate services numbered 37, 38 or 39.

By 1952 it was clear that neither the plans so bravely outlined at the exhibition some years earlier nor these proposed by Mr Fitzpayne in 1948 were likely to come to fruition. The trams were also threatened by the conclusions of the Inglis Report on transport in the Clyde valley, published in December 1951. Incredibly, although Mr Fitzpayne was in attendance at meetings of this committee, there was no representative of Glasgow Corporation among its members, which was entirely biased towards the now nationalised railways and the Scottish Bus Group. Its suggestion that trams should be replaced by other forms of transport 'to ease congestion' was easily refuted by the General Manager, who pointed out that, for traffic flows of over 2,000 passengers per direction/per hour, the tram was still the most economical form of transport.

The Report also suggested that all GCT services running beyond the city boundary should be curtailed at the boundary and the traffic handled by the Scottish Bus Group, as a preliminary to the electrification of the suburban rail network. While nothing came of this in the immediate future, this policy was put into effect once electrification had been agreed in the rail modernisation plan of 1955

and, as most of the services running beyond the boundary were provided by trams, it was the tram system that bore the brunt of the cuts, although in the event certain services, such as that to Burnside, were allowed to remain. It would not have mattered quite so much if the city boundary had followed a logical course, but it did not do so and some of the new termini, such as Hillington Road (the point at which the Renfrew service was curtailed) were in the middle of nowhere, and the Department incurred the cost of providing a service for virtually no revenue. There was also a considerable interval between the withdrawal of the trams and the introduction of electric trains, varying between four years in the case of Airdrie to 18 years for Cambuslang!

Meanwhile there was the problem of the 450 over-age trams. Many of the Standard cars dated back to the first electrification in 1898-99, and by the mid-1950s it was becoming difficult to keep them on the road. The General Manager had first drawn this matter to the attention of the Transport Committee in 1952, but the members were unable to reach any decision and it fell to the workshop staff to contain the problem; this they did mainly by fitting bracing straps to the sides of some of the more decrepit veterans. The problem did not go away, however, although it was partially solved by the purchase of trams from Liverpool, which, with the Clarkston conversion, allowed the scrapping of about 150 Glasgow cars. In 1955 another report recommended the conversion of eight services to motorbus and two to trolleybus operation, and this was accepted first by the Committee then by the full Corporation in April.

From that time it was all downhill and the effects of reduced maintenance on cars and track could be clearly seen from 1957 onwards. The closure of the services running beyond the boundary began with that to Barrhead and Cross Stobs in September 1956 and, despite the Suez crisis, continued in November with those to Cambuslang and Airdrie. The Renfrew and Paisley abandonments were, however, postponed until May 1957, and the period also saw a brief revival of night services on the tram system. Airdrie Town Council went as far as to suggest that the tramway should be re-instated for the duration of the crisis, but the Transport Department had to reply that that would be impossible.

Finally, in June 1957, it was agreed to replace all the remaining trams by motorbuses over a period of 15 to 20 years. Unlike the propaganda used in other cities, there were no great claims that this would result in any improvement in service; in fact, the Convener of the Transport Committee said flatly that the conversion would not have any effect on traffic congestion in the city. It was simply a question of economics; replacement by new trams would have cost more than £11 million, while replacement by motorbuses would cost only £5.5 million. As there was still much life left in the Coronation and Cunarder trams, these would continue in service for a further period after the old cars had been withdrawn, and the final closure would be some time after 1968. However, in August 1958, following a record deficit, it was decided to withdraw all trams by 1963, and in fact the final sad day came on 4 September 1962; with *Telstar* at the top of the charts and Minis in the streets, the trams bowed out.

It was a great tragedy that a fine tramway system, managed by one of Britain's most far-sighted and innovative managers, with a great tradition of service and its own modernised power station, should succumb as it did. No one, apart from the correspondents of the motoring lobby, really wanted to see the trams go, but in the end the prevailing pro-bus mentality of the transport industry and pressure from central government through the nationalised industries combined with economics to force the hand of the Corporation.

No one who remembers the frequency and efficiency of the trams in the 1950s and compares these with today's de-regulated bus industry can doubt that the citizens of Glasgow were the ones who lost out. It is fortunate that the energetic development of the rail system, first with the 'Blue Trains' of the 1960s, then under the policies of Strathclyde Region after 1974, has mitigated the loss.

Today the trams are remembered with as much affection as ever; indeed, they ran again in the city at the Garden Festival of 1988. Plans were drawn up in the early 1990s to build a modern light rail system in Glasgow, which would have been called the Strathclyde Tram. It would have run from Maryhill to Easterhouse, and a great deal of effort and not a little money was spent in consultation on the project. Unfortunately this was a period when Scotland experienced a distinct democratic deficit, being ruled by a government that had no mandate in the country, and it was perhaps not surprising that, when the plans were taken forward under the Private Bills (Scotland) Act of 1936, the parliamentary commissioners appointed by the then Chief Secretary rejected them out of hand. They were not obliged to, and chose not to, give reasons for their decision. Together with the abolition of the Scottish regions, including Strathclyde, by the same government, this debacle ensured that all impetus was lost, and to date there have been so further such plans. At the time of writing it looks as though Edinburgh will beat Glasgow in the matter of bringing trams back to Scotland. All that is left to Glaswegians is to enjoy a nostalgic ride down Memory Lane to Auchenshuggle!

Post-war abandonments in Glasgow

(Figures in brackets indicate last operation of a service)

29.08.48	Broomhouse-Uddingston
23.01.49	Crown Street-Shawfield
20.02.49	Springburn-Netherlee (19)
	Provanmill-Polmadie (2)
03.04.49	Glenfield-Cross Stobs
04.12.49	Clydebank-Duntocher (20)
02.12.51	Sinclair Drive (24A)
15.06.52	Auchenshuggle-Carmyle
05.07.53	Queen's Cross-Clarkston
07.08.55	Shawfield-Rutherglen
29.09.56	Arden-Cross Stobs
03.11.56	Farme Cross-Cambuslang
	Bailieston-Airdrie
	Maryhill-Milngavie
	Maryhill-Dumbreck (40)
11.05.57	Crookston-Elderslie (21)
	(from City Centre)
	Hillington Road-Renfrew Cross
	Renfrew Ferry-Glenfield (28)
16.11.57	Holmlea Road-Kelvinside
	(5, 5A)
16.03.58	Langside-Anniesland (24)
	Springburn-Hillington Road (27)
14.06.58	Millerston-Bellahouston (7)
06.09.58	Springburn-Hillington Road (4)
15.11.58	Mount Florida-Paisley Road
	Toll (12)*
	Anniesland-Farme Cross (17)
	Crookston-Lambhill (22)
	Crookston-Bishopbriggs (32)

04.01.59	Woodlands Road-University
14.03.59	Millerston-Rouken Glen via Giffnock (8)
02.05.59	Springburn and City Circle (33)
06.06.59	Bishopbriggs-Rouken Glen (25)
01.11.59	Riddrie-Scotstoun (6)
	Arden-Kelvingrove (14)
12.03.60	Scotstoun West-Dennistoun (1)
	Blairdardie-Dalmarnock (30)
04.06.60	Park Road-Mosspark (3)
	Park Road-London Road (10)
06.11.60	Tollcross-Broomhouse
	Bailieston-Maryhill (23)
11.03.61	Scotstoun-Springburn (16)
03.06.61	Springburn-Burnside (18)
	Springburn-Shawfield (18A)
22.10.61	Maryhill-Tollcross (29)
10.03.62	Anderston Cross-Bailieston (15)
02.06.62	Clydebank-Dalmarnock (26)
01.09.62	Dalmuir West-Auchenshuggle (9) (Special workings Anderston Cross Auchenshuggle operated 2-4 September)

* There were special workings of the 12 to Govan and Shieldhall, mainly for shipyard workers, and these ceased on the previous day, thus marking the end of the trams in the formerly independent burgh of Govan, which had until 1912 owned, but not operated, the lines in its area.

THE CREWS:
THE VIEW FROM THE BACK PLATFORM

The crews, no doubt, saw it all. Life on the back platform was hard – it involved standing for up to eight hours at a time, carrying a heavy ticket-issuing machine around one's neck, with a bag full of copper penny and halfpenny coins over the shoulder, and all for a weekly wage of around £11 in 1960. The fare structure of the Glasgow system had been greatly simplified in the 1920s to combat competition from motor buses, and although there were fairly frequent increases in the post-war years, the scales did not change. From 1955 these were 2½d for one or two stages, 4d for three or four and 6d for longer journeys; the minimum fare was (quite needlessly) increased to 3d at the time of the Suez crisis in 1956, to prevent invidious comparison with the new fares on the buses.

The crews wore a uniform of bottle green with red piping. Male staff had peaked caps that were almost always worn, while women drivers and conductresses latterly wore a type of forage cap – Glasgow did not allow the wearing of headscarves. The standard of turn-out was high and anyone reporting for duty in non-uniform clothing would not have been allowed out on the road.

Here we see the smartly attired crew of Cunarder 1324 at Mosspark terminus in June 1960, a few days before the abandonment of service 3. The conductor carries an 'Ultimate' ticket machine, first introduced at Newlands depot in 1948, and a stout leather bag, probably already well filled with copper penny coins. Both men wear regulation black shoes; plimsolls were not allowed and trainers had not been invented! The driver's time card is propped against the windscreen. Unfortunately the names of the crew have not been recorded.

There was no special summer uniform, not even white cap covers, and on hot days the heavy serge material could make life very uncomfortable, even though male staff were then allowed to work in shirt sleeves. Despite the heat of the golden summer of 1959, the crew of car 76 wear full regulation uniform while taking a break at the terminus of service 16 in Elmvale Street, Springburn.

Even allowing for changes in the value of money since then, these fares were very low, especially for the longer journeys. However, much of the traffic was short-distance, so the amount of copper in the conductor's money bag increased very quickly. It was unusual to tender more than a shilling for a fare, and to proffer a half-crown (2s 6d) was to risk a ribald comment, an enquiry as to possible confusion of the No 4 with the Bank of Scotland; it was quite unheard of to tender even a 10 shilling note, let alone £1. Tokens, made from a kind of bakelite, were sold, but were intended mainly for the convenience of employers whose staff had to make journeys in the course of their work and who might otherwise be tempted to pauchle (fiddle) their tram fare.

The main problem for a conductor was not remembering fares but fare stages. These were located about every half-mile, and on a long service such as the 9 there could be 20 separate stages. Mostly these were named after intermediate streets, but on some of the longer roads, such as London Road, stages were named after the number of a nearby tenement. No 181 Castle Street and 1 New City Road were among several closes (entries to tenements) celebrated in this way.

On the window of the platform there was a little red box, with the invitation to place uncollected fares in it. This box was never used, a tribute more to the thoroughness of the conducting staff than to the honesty of Glaswegians.

Conductors spent three days at a training school at Govan before being allocated to a depot and being sent out on the road with an experienced member of staff to learn the practicalities. After a few more days they were

This smart line-up in front of 1247 marks the departure of the last trams from Dennistoun depot on 6 November 1960. *W. J. Guthrie*

on their own. Work could begin as early as 5am and finish as late as 1am, after which a call at an all-night bakery for a roll or teabread was very welcome. On many days split shifts were worked, and it was usual for conducting staff to live fairly near their depot, to allow a return home between turns on the road. A conductor could expect to work on several services during one day; it was quite common to work one trip on, perhaps, service 14 on an elderly Standard before transferring to the luxury of a Cunarder on the 3 for the rest of the day.

The 3 was probably a favourite with the staff, since the passengers on the Mosspark section tended to be extremely polite, while in the other direction the tram would be full of students with essays or exams on their minds and thus not inclined to give trouble. On a modern car, a friendly conductress would sometimes let you sit in the rear driving cabin, a quiet spot for a bit of frantic last-minute revision. In return for their service, the trams found their way into several student songs, and at the end of term a tramload of students

could be heard assuring the world in general that:

'You can't go to Heaven on a number 3 car,
'Cause the number 3 car don't go that far...'

Conductors could expect to have some unusual duties to break the monotony of frequent trips to Arden or Bishopbriggs. A favourite was the Sunday special service from Cross Stobs inward to Spiersbridge, essentially a Barrhead local service and generally not well patronised. Riding the reserved track through the Renfrewshire countryside on a sunny summer day could be most pleasant, a total contrast to Castle Street at 6am on a December morning, and at double pay too!

But Sundays were by no means always quiet. In the days when the family car was still an unheard-of luxury for even relatively affluent Glaswegians, the main way to get to one of the city's many fine parks was by tram, and services such as the 8, which served Hogganfield Loch, could see full trams for most of the day. In winter the Sunday traffic

took a different aspect, when most passengers were bound either for church or, later in the day, for tea at Aunt Maggie's.

There was also heavy late-evening traffic, particularly on Fridays and Saturdays, when the theatres and cinemas closed. The smell of a poke (packet) of chips, often shared between a couple who were 'gaun' steady', mingled with tobacco smoke and beer to produce a quite

Left Uses of the window at the end of the upper deck – the conductor of car 170, working service 10 at Hyndland in June 1960, prepares to pull over the bow collector as the car moves forward on to the crossover. Glasgow did not have automatic trolley reversers and some encouragement was needed.

Below left A disappointed queue of housewives in headscarves and wee boys in school caps and short trousers look on while the crew of a Standard prepare to reverse the tram at Shettleston crossover on a thoroughly miserable November afternoon in 1960. While the driver changes the points with the point iron – which was normally kept behind the used ticket box – the conductor, having set the final destination blind at 'Parkhead', searches for an appropriate indication in the lower blind, which normally showed a suitable 'via' point; that word had been carried on the blinds before the war, but had been deleted in 1940 to confuse any invaders, and was not re-instated after hostilities ended.

Below Shortly after the photograph on page 14 was taken, the 16 service was cut back to its former terminus at Keppochill Road, where Coronation 1251 reverses in August 1960. The driver sets the points for the crossover,

distinctive aroma on the upper deck. These nights could see some boisterous passengers, but conductors and perhaps even more conductresses normally had no trouble reducing unwanted vocalists to silence. Really hard cases were crushed by a threat to get the driver. Assaults on staff were rare and seizure of the day's takings unheard of.

The conducting staff viewed their passengers tolerantly on the whole, though they were sometimes moved to comment aloud after a particularly difficult turn of duty. Normally this was done in broad Glasgow, occasionally in broad Donegal, both unintelligible to visitors from England, but in later days it could be in Bengali or Urdu. The conductress of a No 40 viewed the alighting of the last of many mothers with noisy children with obvious relief, then, shaking her head, announced to the remaining passengers, 'Ah never seen so much weans (children) in a' ma days. Ah wun'er whit they get up tae in Maryhill. Right "Hooswives' Choice" this road, so it is.'

Prams could be carried on the driver's platform, but in the poorer areas of the city it was still usual to see a mother carrying a baby

while the conductress of GCT Leyland bus L284 on the left helps an elderly passenger on board. This view shows the type of stop signs used for buses and trams – yellow in the former case, red in the latter.

Right One of the members of staff who contributed much to the smooth running of the system was the depot gateman, whose responsibility it was to assign incoming trams to the correct lye in the depot for their next turn of duty. The gateman at Partick has set the road for Standard 681 in August 1960.

Left The driver of car 468, working a peak-hour extension of service 12, holds out his arm to indicate a right turn as he swings into the terminal siding at Linthouse.

in a shawl wrapped around her shoulder. Towards the end of the trams the first 'baby buggies' made their appearance and obliging staff would stow these on the platform, often propped against the resistance box. This box was warm and sometimes could become really hot, in which case the plastic handles of the pushchair melted.

In the late 1940s Glasgow Corporation embarked on a campaign to improve the conduct of its passengers. This involved Mungo, a cartoon character who was, it said, Glasgow's Good Citizen and clearly represented the kind of passenger the Corporation hoped to have, but seldom did. He was rather like London Transport's Billy Brown, but had more of a sense of humour. Mungo, passengers were assured, was no queue-jumper, but he did board the tram or

bus promptly, this panegyric being illustrated by a cartoon of a passenger flying in through a top-deck window. Furthermore, Mungo did not stand on the platform and did not sit on it either! There was also a wee Mungo who, when the tram or bus was busy, sat on his daddy's knee – he too would be a good citizen. Mungo had a fairly long innings, but no noticeable effect on the habits of passengers, who continued in their naughty ways. When he finally passed into retirement, he was replaced by a lass who had strong views about litter and was called Sal Vage, but she did not last so long.

From the conductor's point of view, all Glasgow's trams were relatively easy to work. Platforms were wide and there was ample space to stand aside from the stream of passengers and yet be able to supervise

boarding and alighting and, if necessary, to issue warnings such as 'Wan dug on each deck'. (Dogs could be a problem on services that passed near a greyhound racing stadium.) The modern cars afforded the conductor the chance to use the front staircase to gain access to the upper deck, without retracing her or his steps through the lower saloon.

Apart from collection of fares, a conductor had to be prepared to reset the circuit breaker when that was on the rear platform; on the Standards this was a black box fixed to the ceiling of the platform and, if the driver accelerated too quickly or forgot to cut off power at certain places, this would switch out with a loud bang, cutting off the current supply. Drivers who did this when their conductor was changing half a crown on the upper deck quickly became unpopular! A driver might also request his conductor to 'Gie the bow a chug'; this cry was heard when the collector seemed not to be making proper contact with the overhead and involved lowering the window at the rear end of the upper deck and pulling hard on the rope until

the bow collector ran more smoothly. The bow collector was heavier than it looked.

Not all conducting duties involved passengers. Trams bound for scrapping at Elderslie depot carried a conductor, as did trams running to or from Coplawhill Works, and as late as 1954 a conductor could have the pleasure of conducting a totally new tram on its way into service.

In these days of driver-only operation of buses, it is easy to forget the help that was regularly offered by the women and men in green on the back platform of the tram, but it must have been valued by many elderly passengers and by mothers handicapped by a large brood of children! It was not long after the demise of the trams that the conductor followed them into oblivion, and many people lamented the passing of both institutions with equal regret.

This section has been based on notes made by Richard Wiseman, Editor of Tramway Review, *who worked as a conductor in Glasgow in 1954.*

ROUTES AND SERVICES

Cowcaddens, Hope Street and Oswald Street

One of the main north-south arteries of the system was that formed by Hope Street and Oswald Street, which the trams had to share with buses. After 1945 it was served for much of its length by services 4, 21, 22, 27 and 40, these being joined between Argyle and Bothwell Streets by the 10, 17 and 18/18A. In 1953 the 29 was re-routed via Hope Street, while in the following year the 21 became southbound only.

Below left The vista of Cowcaddens, looking west from Maitland Street, has been totally erased since this photograph was taken in November 1958. Cunarder 1350 is working on service 22, followed by a GCT AEC Regent, while a Mk 2 Ford Consul is parked at the kerb. To the left of the tram is one of the Easiphit shoe shops, which were to be found all over the city. As can be seen from the overhead, trolleybuses also operated here. Today the area is a wilderness of roads.

Right The north end of Hope Street is dominated by the Theatre Royal. In the later days of the trams this was the home of Scottish Television, but it has now reverted to 'live' theatre, as the base for Scottish Opera, presenting a range of operas in marked contrast to the annual one-week visits to the city by the Carl Rosa Opera Company in the 1950s. Cunarder 1342 on service 22 turns into Cowcaddens in November 1958, followed by a fine Rolls-Royce.

Below The junction with Sauchiehall Street always provided heavy pedestrian traffic, and still does today. In August 1960 Cunarder 1359 is flanked at the lights by two Hillman Huskies and followed by a GCT Leyland PD2.

Left On the opposite side of Hope Street looking north, we see not only the almost unchanged frontage of Watt Brothers, but also Standard 1051 following ex-Liverpool car 1010 down to the Sauchiehall Street junction.

Below On a typically 'dreich' (wet, dull and generally miserable) afternoon in November 1960, a Cunarder follows a Ford Anglia or Popular downhill to the junction with St Vincent Street. On a day such as this, the excellent interior lighting certainly brightened the scene.

Above On the same day 283 is about to turn left into Bothwell Street. Behind is the then grimy facade of the Central Hotel, designed for the Caledonian Railway in 1884 by Sir Rowand Anderson and now beautifully restored, but no longer a railway hotel. By 1960 the trams had to compete with much more traffic than formerly, and the conductor is signalling a left turn to the driver of the Ford following behind. A Morris Traveller estate car is also turning into Bothwell Street, followed by a Messerschmidt 'bubble car', another Ford and an Austin taxi. Two hardened jay-walkers make for the western pavement.

Right A rather quieter scene looking north from Central station at Easter 1959. Former Liverpool car 1048 is followed by an Austin taxi, with traditional open luggage space beside the driver, and a new GCT Leyland PD2.

The junction of Hope Street and Argyle Street was one of the city's busiest, at least until the lines via Oswald Street (right foreground) were abandoned. As can be seen here, pointwork on abandoned lines was removed to give a smoother ride to remaining passengers. It is April 1961 and football fans are offered a 'Wembley Special' return fare of 80 shillings (£4) by British Railways. Car 1217 is bound for Maryhill, while another Coronation waits under the 'Hielanman's Umbrella' – the bridge carrying Central station over Argyle Street.

In the post-war years some Standards were rebuilt with flush side panels and tail lights, and on King George V Bridge one such car, 143, jostles for road space with bus L62, followed by a smart Austin A55 Cambridge. As yet there are no electric wires on the railway bridge leading into Glasgow Central, where in August 1958 all trains were still worked by steam.

Renfield Street, Union Street and Jamaica Street

These three streets, forming another of the main north-south axes in the city centre, were, with Argyle Street, the busiest part of the tramway system. Buses had once run there, but from 1946 to 1957 the tram reigned supreme; in the mid-1950s there was, between St Vincent and Sauchiehall Streets, a car in each direction every 12½ seconds. Until 1953 ten services used the northern section of Renfield Street, and in that year the number was increased to 11 with the diversion of the 23 from West Nile Street, while from 1954 inbound trams on the 21 used the southern part to reach their new terminus in St Vincent Street. The combined frequency of trams seemed to discourage such motorists as there were, and Renfield Street was virtually a tram/pedestrian precinct. Operation was efficient and many stopping places had double stops to segregate passengers for different services. The main obstacle to the free flow of traffic was not the trams but the numerous traffic lights, of which there were four sets between Sauchiehall Street and St Vincent Place alone. Today only Swanston Street in Melbourne offers a tram service comparable to Renfield Street in its heyday.

This view looking south into Renfield Street from Sauchiehall Street was taken around midday on 2 May 1958. Behind tram 217 is one of the Albion buses used by the Corporation Education Department to take children to and from special schools. Part of the facade of Renfield Street United Presbyterian Church is just visible on the right; it was built in 1848 to a design by the architect James Brown and demolished in 1965.

Left By March 1959 'No Waiting' signs had appeared in the central area, although these seem to have been ignored by the drivers of at least three cars, parked at the shops in the building of the Bank of Scotland; the car on the extreme left is a Mercedes. Car 217 working on service 8 is followed by a Dodge lorry and partnered by a Volkswagen 'Beetle' with a rather unattractive Glasgow registration. Today the scene is little changed, though the bank building has been cleaned and subsequently vacated by the bank; at present it is derelict, awaiting a new owner. Off to the right the premises of the former fruit and vegetable shop run by Malcolm Campbell are now occupied by the sandwich bar chain Prêt à Manger, a type of shop unknown in 1959, when most Glaswegians still went home for lunch.

Below Looking north up Union Street in the days of completely haphazard parking! Two drivers have parked face to face, while on the other side a Bedford lorry unloads goods outside Birrell's sweet shop. A new Cunarder tram, in the first paint style applied to this class, heads south. None of the buildings seen in this view have changed greatly, although the Cadoro (right) has been rebuilt after a fire and now houses a supermarket. *Commercial postcard, author's collection*

A rather later view, from the opposite side of the street, shows Standard 404 stopping outside the Union Street entrance of Glasgow Central station on the morning of 13 March 1958. Already service 5 has been converted, and one of the replacement buses, a Daimler, lurks behind. To the left of the tram is one of Carswell's shops, then a well-known outfitter in the city. The lady shoppers are neatly attired in hats.

Saturday 4 June 1960 was the last day of operation of service 3, and thus of trams along these streets, and car 1220 is seen among the shoppers at the junction of Jamaica and Union Streets with Argyle Street. The right-angled crossing from this junction survives today at the National Tramway Museum. The intersection is now a centre for the fast food industry, there being four such outlets, one on each of the corner sites.

This view looking north from Gordon Street dates from just at the end of the Second World War, when buses still shared the street with trams. Some of the trams still have white-painted fenders from blackout days, and the buses have green roofs. Behind the Standard on service 24 can be seen one of the single-deckers from service 20, probably on its way to the Works; these trams did not normally operate in the city centre. *W. J. Guthrie collection*

Argyle Street

For many Glaswegians this was the most typical tramway street. Until late in the conversion programme, no buses ran in the central part of the street and the constant stream of trams – there were seven basic services – was a prominent feature, together with stores such as Lewis's and Arnott's.

Right Cunarder 1305 is seen just west of St Enoch Square in June 1960, towards the end of operation of service 10.

Below The part of Argyle Street east of Queen Street is now a pedestrian precinct, but in November 1960 car 1133 shares the street with, on the left, an Austin A30 and a Mk 2 Ford Zephyr convertible passing a parked Ford Prefect, while on the right is a parked Austin Hereford, and a jay-walker.

'City Centre'

This rather vague destination may have originated during the war years as a security measure, but its continued use was unhelpful to the travelling public, as the actual locations could be anything up to a mile apart! Most commonly it referred to Anderston Cross, the heart of the former burgh of that name.

On a foggy afternoon in the autumn of 1956, Coronation 1251 awaits departure for Airdrie, while on the extreme right a man pushes a hand cart along a traffic-free street. The shop fronts may have been uninviting and the tenements dull, but these were not slums and did not deserve to be obliterated in one of the worst comprehensive redevelopment schemes of the 1960s.

St Vincent Street was a more accurate city centre terminus, though it was used as such only from October 1954 to May 1957, by service 21, and here we see car 37 taking a layover on 20 April of the latter year. Today the surrounding buildings are cleaner, but otherwise unaltered, and the police box was removed just after the first edition of this book was published; however, motorcycle and sidecar combinations are no longer seen.

Around Charing Cross

To the north of Charing Cross two Cunarders pass in Woodlands Road in May 1960. Just visible behind the tram on the left is one of the tea-rooms of James Craig, at one time numerous throughout the city. The buildings on the left survive, but those behind the tram on the right have gone and a pedestrian footbridge crosses the M8 at this point to link Renfrew Street with the western end of Sauchiehall Street.

Left An unidentified Standard hurries through Charing Cross on an October afternoon in 1959 – the motorcycle combination that has cut in, in hot pursuit of the Mk 1 Ford Consul, has prevented the recording of the tram's number. Note that the rider is not wearing any kind of head protection! In the block behind the tram was the tea-room of William Skinner, established in the 1890s and scarcely altered in 1959; it was noted as an establishment of solid elegance and had a particular reputation for currant bread. It closed soon afterwards and the building has since been demolished. The single west-to-north curve in the foreground was used only for depot workings, but Charing Cross was one of the busiest junctions on the system. Today a slip road to the motorway cuts across at the point from which this photograph was taken.

Below Cunarder 1322 heads south on service 16, passing Glasgow Boys' High School in Elmbank Street in August 1960. Behind on Sauchiehall Street is the former Beresford Hotel, Glasgow's largest Art Deco building, erected originally for the Empire Exhibition of 1938 and by the time of this photograph already converted to a student hall of residence. The box on the right houses tramway feeder cables, while on the pole beyond can be seen one of the circular discs put up by the GCT with the exhortation to 'Drive cautiously'. How far these influenced drivers was debatable!

At the triangular junction Coronation 1189 is waved out of Elmbank Street into St Vincent Street by a policeman on point duty, while an Austin taxi makes for the city via Bothwell Street. Today the buildings on the right have gone, that of the Ford dealer being replaced by an office block. The junction, no longer triangular, is controlled by traffic lights, and it would be dangerous for anyone to stand in the middle of the road today.

In another view of the junction from St Vincent Street, taken in November 1958, Standard 852 turns into Bothwell Street in front of a GCT AEC Regent, while on the right a Central SMT Leyland PD2 heads for Balloch, Loch Lomond. The building behind the tram and beyond the car showroom housed Glasgow's Ear, Nose and Throat hospital.

Parliamentary Road

Above left Forming the eastern extension of Sauchiehall Street, Parliamentary Road is one of the streets that have since completely disappeared. In this view, taken on the evening of 12 March 1959, car 1167 picks up a few passengers at the stop immediately east of Buchanan Street. It is on a short working of service 8 to Riddrie, while the car behind is running through to Millerston. Just visible to the left is the front of the 'Canasta', one of Glasgow's first coffee bars in 1956.

Above right Sunshine after rain: car 459 is reflected in the asphalt paving just east of Dundas Street on a short working to Newlands on 26 February 1959, while an SMT Bristol Lodekka bus lurks in the background. Buchanan Street bus station now occupies the site and the area is totally unrecognisable.

At the junction of Parliamentary Road and Castle Street there was an unusual track layout with one-way working by services 6 and 8. Here car 89 turns into Castle Street on service 6 in October 1959. Behind the tram can be seen the premises of a doctor's surgery, of somewhat uninviting aspect, and the equally gloomy facade of the National Bank of Scotland Ltd. Today the area is a desolate waste of motorway junctions, devoid of any sign of human habitation, gloomy or otherwise!

Junctions

As befitted a large system, Glasgow had many busy junctions, both in the inner city and in the suburban area.

Above left Eglinton Toll, in the south of the city, had formerly been a three-way junction for outward-bound trams, but as early as 1946 increasing traffic congestion had enforced rationalisation, and services via Victoria Road (to the right) were diverted to leave Eglinton Street at Turiff Street and the tracks at the Toll were separated by a barrier.

Above right Looking in towards the city from Eglinton Toll, with the barrier on the right, Coronation 1258 heads out for Merrylee on 5 November 1959. The bar in the right background shows one of the Art Deco facades with which many Glasgow bars and cafes were modernised in the 1930s.

Right Parkhead Cross in the eastern suburbs was a complex five-way junction whose points were controlled from a signal tower. On the wet Saturday afternoon of 5 November 1960 a Standard tram turns out of Springfield Road into Gallowgate, prior to making a short working to Shettleston on service 15.

Below A less complex but still busy layout was that at the intersection of St Vincent and Argyle Streets in the west. By August 1960 the street lighting has been converted to sodium, but the barber's shop on the left still displays the traditional red and white striped pole. The buildings on the left have gone but those on the right, now beautifully cleaned, survive. Kilmarnock Bogie 1119 follows an Austin A40 westwards along Argyle Street towards Partick.

Above St George's Cross was another busy five-way junction, which was also served by a Subway station. The latter still exists, but most of the surrounding area has been redeveloped out of existence, largely to make way for the M8 motorway. In August 1960 the Cross was still a busy traffic and commercial centre. The department store of Wood and Selby occupied premises on both sides of St George's Road, along which a Cunarder proceeds bound for Springburn on service 16, while a Morris Minor follows a Ford round into Great Western Road.

Left The Round Toll was originally a tollgate on the Garscube Turnpike, until tolls were abolished in the 1870s and the round tollhouse demolished. The name survived, however, and on 8 November 1958 car 240 clears the junction bound for Lambhill on service 22. Between this point and Cowcaddens, the trams shared the road with trolleybuses on service 105, but despite official reservations they seem to have co-existed happily enough. The tracks in the foreground took services 16 and 31 into St George's Road. Just visible behind the tram in the gloom are a trolleybus and a couple of motorbuses.

Above right Glasgow Cross had lost something of its importance as a tramway junction when the services in High Street were converted to trolleybus operation in 1949. Post-war views of trams on this section are very rare, and this view of Standard 51 probably dates from around 1938. Working southbound on the 'white' service to Mount Florida (later numbered 19), it is passing an early petrol tanker in the Saltmarket. *W. J. Guthrie collection*

Right The same view, taken about ten years later, shows one of the new trolleybuses in original livery and displaying on the rear panel the London-style trolleybus roundel. These were removed soon after due to objections from London Transport. *Author's collection*

GLASGOW CROSS

GLASGOW CROSS

The remaining junction at Glasgow Cross was that of the lines to Gallowgate and London Road. In June 1959 ex-Liverpool 1031 from the former has given way to 1137 from the latter – but was the driver of the van that has just overtaken the Green Goddess aware of this? On the left is a Vauxhall Cresta and the Tron Steeple, all that remains of the Tron church, burned down in 1793 and rebuilt apart from its steeple. Pedestrian arches were cut through it in the mid-19th century.

The home of the Standards: Services 1 and 30

The former green services 1 and 30 could lay claim to being the oldest in Glasgow, since they incorporated parts of the original horse-car route of 1872. They served a variety of areas, in terms of both social conditions and architectural styles, but by 1960 their chief claim to fame was that they were still worked entirely by Standard cars. More modern cars could not work on the 30 due to clearance problems at Parkhead Cross, while the few Coronations that had formerly appeared on the 1 were used elsewhere after 1957. The passing of these services in March 1960 really was the beginning of the end.

Half a mile from Dalmarnock terminus in the east, trams on the 30 turned right into Springfield Road, to which point the 1 was sometimes extended. Car 394 has obviously fooled the drivers of the following two Austins, who have assumed that it will go on and have pulled in behind it; instead it is preparing to reverse, and some tricky manoeuvres are required! The conductor frantically winds the indicator blind, but so far has turned up only 'Langloan', a point on the former Airdrie route, closed in 1956.

Left Further along Springfield Road, at the crossing with London Road, a surprising number of private cars are in evidence, including several Austins, a Ford and, on the left of the picture, a stylish Alvis, whose driver clearly believes in cutting corners as he turns right into London Road. The coach is from the fleet of Dodd's of Troon, Ayrshire. Standard 245 heads north-west for Scotstoun West on a Saturday in February 1960.

Below left In Dennistoun, the normal eastern terminus of service 1, car 658 is seen on Duke Street on 13 March 1959. By this date 658 was one of the oldest trams in service, having completed 59 years on the city's streets. There were still 32 cinemas open in the city in that year and, as many of the programmes were double-billed and often changed mid-week, Glaswegians were offered a wide choice of film. One of the smallest cinemas was The Granada, behind the tram, which is showing *The Safecracker*, a 1958 film starring Ray Milland, and a western of the same year, *Saddle the Wind*, starring Robert Taylor.

Right Turning to the western end of the routes, car 812, now preserved at Crich, waits at the traffic lights at Park Road, Kelvinbridge, heading for Blairdardie in March 1960. A Morris-Commercial mail van stands alongside, while in the distance a classic Wolseley is parked in the side street, Lansdowne Gardens.

The section of Great Western Road between Kelvindale and Anniesland had a reserved track for trams, but the rails were laid in ordinary stone setts, rather than in ballast. One of Glasgow's red and yellow traffic markers, sometimes known as 'pillars of fire', can be seen on the left as car 268 works a peak-hour duty to Yoker.

Car 9 stops at Hillhead in March 1960. The advertisement on the dash is for the *Evening Citizen*, one of the three evening papers then published in the city, of which only the *Evening Times* survives today. The driver, smiling cheerfully at the camera, is one of the those who had arrived from the Indian sub-continent to settle in Glasgow in the late 1950s, many of whom found employment on the trams and the Subway.

The last extension of the Glasgow system was that from Knightswood Cross to Blairdardie, opened on 31 July 1949. It was on a neat reserved track, running through one of Glasgow's 'garden city' housing schemes, laid out from 1924 onwards; today many of the houses are in private ownership. Car 156 approaches the terminus in March 1960, with only a Sunbeam Rapier for company.

At Anniesland Cross a gyratory traffic system operated from the 1930s, with which the trams coped perfectly well, despite suggestions to the contrary often made by the motoring lobby. Car 812 is again seen in this view taken in March 1959.

Springburn

This was Glasgow's railway suburb, having at one time accommodated the works of five locomotive builders within its boundaries. Even in 1958 the North British Locomotive Company was still very active and had begun to diversify into the construction of diesel locomotives for British Railways, while BR itself maintained Cowlairs Works and a substantial depot at St Rollox. Today most rail activity has ceased, although electric trains serve the area.

The 33 was Glasgow's only circular service and the trams showed the same destination in both directions and at all points on the journey, thus sparing conductors the need to change the destination blinds! On the anti-clockwise circle, Standard 477 turns out of Springburn against a background of typical tenements and small shops, including two surgeries.

This is the centre of Springburn at Keppochill Road in 1958. On the left the main shop is that of D. M. Hoey, outfitter, a firm that has only recently gone out of business; next to it is an ironmonger, while just visible on the left are a butcher and a tobacconist. Car 4 is working on service 25.

Running in the opposite direction, 522 turns into Springburn. While the term 'juggernaut' was not then in use to describe heavy lorries, the two passing behind the tram would certainly have merited that nickname when this photograph was taken in May 1959.

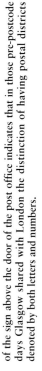

Above left On a short working of service 25, Standard 108 takes a layover at the siding in Elmvale Street, Springburn, in May 1959. While the billboards outside the newsagent's shop were probably proclaiming the policies of the Macmillan Government, the *Evening Citizen*, as part of the circulation war with its rivals, was apparently preparing to fight the battles of the First World War over again ('Did the brass hats send an army to die in Flanders fields?'); at that time many Glasgow people would still have vivid memories of that conflict. The 'N' at the end

of the sign above the door of the post office indicates that in those pre-postcode days Glasgow shared with London the distinction of having postal districts denoted by both letters and numbers.

Above right Coming south from Springburn, trams encountered an unusual track layout at the junction of Parliamentary Road and Castle Street (see also page 35), where Standard 64 reverses in Monkland Street on a short working of the 8. This conductor has clearly mastered the art of reading the destination blind upside-down! The distant advertisements behind the tram proclaim the merits of Bristol cigarettes and the classic Cadbury's Dairy Milk chocolate.

Along the 18

The 18 was a former 'white' car service and linked Springburn with Rutherglen by a somewhat circuitous route. It is doubtful if anyone save the occasional enthusiast made the complete journey, but the trams were busy with intermediate traffic. Although running beyond the city boundary, the 18 was not pruned in 1956/57 and in fact survived, together with the associated 18A, until 3 June 1961.

The line passed beneath the aqueduct of the Forth & Clyde Canal at Bilsland Drive, and at times it was possible to see a Clyde 'puffer' floating above a Glasgow tram. In the first view (*right*), taken from the canal bank, Coronation 1155 heads towards the bridge, while in the second Cunarder 1371 is followed by a GCT Leyland bus, travelling in the opposite direction in August 1960.

Above Northbound Standard 286, the first of the 'hex dash' design, approaches the turn into Elmbank Street at the end of Bothwell Street (seen also on page 33). The driver is holding out his right arm to indicate a turn to the driver of the Austin A55 pick-up following behind. The building on the left has since been replaced by a modern office block and the street is a dead end at this point.

Below On a dull and drizzly afternoon in November 1960, an unidentified Coronation slows to a stop outside Wendy's tea-room in Bothwell Street, followed by a Triumph Herald and Austin A55. In the background a Central SMT Leyland PD2 has just left Waterloo Street bus station bound for one of the services along Dumbarton Road.

Coronation 1221, outward bound to Burnside, approaches the junction at Farme Cross in April 1961, followed by a Mk 2 Ford Consul and a Central SMT Leyland PD3. The tracks diverging to the right are the remains of the Cambuslang branch, which, since 1956, had terminated at a point about 200 yards from the junction.

The gable ends of the tenements were a favourite location for advertisements, and those to the right of the bus invite consumers to 'Unzipp a banana' and drink Usher's Amber Ale, inform us that 'People like Players', and recommend that they should buy SCWS (Co-operative) goods.

Clarkston

The extension from Cathcart to Clarkston was planned before 1914 and was opened to Netherlee after the outbreak of war. Work continued for a time on the next stage, but shortage of labour and materials (despite the employment of Belgian refugees) finally led to a postponement, and it was not completed until 1921. In the post-1945 period there were two services, the 13 to Maryhill and (later) Milngavie, and the 5/5A to Kelvinside. The latter, serving the shopping centre of Victoria Road en route to the heart of the city, was the busier, but when the 13 was replaced by trolleybuses in 1953, the 5/5A had to be cut back to Holmlea Road and a useful link was broken. These four views, taken on 30 June and 7 July 1953, show the terminus before and after the conversion.

This page Standard car 401 awaits departure to Kelvinside on service 5A, while the second slightly blurred view shows Coronation 1148 on the 5A sharing the terminus with Standard 723 on the 13.

Above right Trolleybus TD14, a Daimler with London-style bodywork, displays the original attractive, but slightly impractical, livery of green lower and cream upper panels, with cream roof and two orange bands between the upper and lower decks. As yet no advertisements are carried, and the city crest is prominent on the upper panels. To distinguish them from motorbus services, the destination blinds on the trolleybuses had white lettering on a green background. It was not easy to read even when new, and became almost invisible with age!

Right Trolleybus TG9, one of the Weymann-bodied Sunbeams bought for this conversion, shows the revised livery of green window surrounds and a green roof.

The 8 and 25

Linking the affluent northern suburbs of Riddrie and Bishopbriggs with their southern counterparts of Eastwood and Giffnock via industrial Springburn was one of the original 'red' services, which became the 8 and 8A in 1938 and was split into the 8 and 25 in 1943.

Car 145 and BUT trolleybus TB54 share Millerston terminus, north-east of the city, in March 1959. The original, standard terminal layout of a double track with a facing crossover had been replaced by a single track when the 7 was converted to trolleybus, to provide the clearance required by the Ministry of Transport.

Right At Riddrie the trams climbed steeply to cross the Monkland Canal. Coronation 1169 follows a sturdy Glasgow-built Albion lorry over the bridge.

Below Both services ran to several of the city's many fine parks and in summer carried much excursion traffic. But only one family has ventured out to Hogganfield Loch on a chilly March day in 1959, as car 65 passes on the 8 service.

The low bridge in Castle Street had been the reason for the use of single-deckers on Glasgow's first electric service in 1898. The roadway was later both lowered and widened, but the tram tracks remained off-centre to the end. Looking north, car 79 passes two small boys, who have obviously scorned to use the pavement on the other side of the road, and a fine specimen of an early electric lamp.

As has already been mentioned, Springburn was the centre of locomotive building in Glasgow and many of the workers employed in the industry lived in tenements like those seen in this photograph. A Standard car picks up some passengers while a Morris Commercial van waits behind. The premises of the wine merchant to the right are more than a little different from those of the modern off-licence!

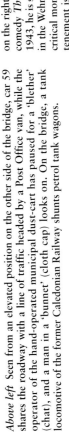

Above left Seen from an elevated position on the other side of the bridge, car 59 shares the roadway with a line of traffic headed by a Post Office van, while the operator of the hand-operated municipal dust-cart has paused for a 'blether' (chat), and a man in a 'bunnet' (cloth cap) looks on. On the bridge, a tank locomotive of the former Caledonian Railway shunts petrol tank wagons.

Above right Looking up Castle Street in March 1959, car 464 is inbound on service 8, while behind are a northbound Coronation tram and a bus; just visible on the right is a trolleybus. The Carlton cinema is showing the Norman Wisdom comedy *The Square Peg*, in which, dropped accidentally behind enemy lines in 1943, he is saved from trouble by his striking resemblance to a high-ranking officer in the Wehrmacht and his ability to sing (with Hattie Jacques) an opera duet at a critical moment! The second feature is *Fury Unleashed*. On the gable end of the tenement is another timeless advertisement (for Heinz beans) with, below, an offering of the Egg Marketing Board, suggesting that the larder was empty without eggs. Few households in the area would have had a refrigerator.

Above In the south, both services passed through some streets of fine tenements. At Greenview Street in Shawlands, a pedestrian overtakes a Mk 1 Ford Zephyr in his anxiety to catch car 103, while a coal merchant's lorry turns out of the side street. Apart from Omo, now only to be found on the continent, all the products advertised on the hoarding are still available.

Left Pollokshaws was a separate burgh until 1912, and even in the late 1950s the Main Street retained something of a village atmosphere. Here again the tracks had not been moved when the roadway was widened, and any motorist foolhardy enough to overtake Cunarder 1317 (on service 14) would have been in for a nasty shock, as a tram was just about to pass in the opposite direction.

Right The short branch of the 25 along Boydstone Road to Carnwadric, although running through a pre-war housing scheme, was not opened until 20 February 1949. It left the main line at Thornliebank station, where Cunarder 1322 waits in June 1959 while the driver changes the points.

Below Car 4 passes a parked Ford on the branch, just west of the junction on 5 June 1959; behind it is one of rather inhospitable shelters, which were painted to match the trams.

On a hot day in July 1955, Cunarder 1341 awaits home-going passengers from the adjacent park at Rouken Glen terminus.

The Paisley and Govan services

These services still showed traces of their independent origin, the lines in Paisley having been operated until 1923 by the local Paisley District Company, while the Govan lines had been owned by that authority until it was absorbed into Glasgow in 1912. There was also inter-running with goods trains to and from the shipyards, a facility that had originally caused the adoption of Glasgow's odd track gauge of 4ft 7¾in.

In a tranquil scene at Elderslie terminus after the evening rush hour in May 1952, car 194, on service 32, is nearest the camera, and there's not a motor vehicle in sight!

To accommodate special cars for the Babcock & Wilcox factory, a lengthy siding was laid in Porterfield Road, Renfrew, capable of holding up to a dozen trams. On 23 April 1957 Standard 70 prepares to leave the siding on an un-numbered cross-suburban working to Bridgeton, using the tracks of services 4 and 7. The *Scotsman* newspaper was then mounting an advertising campaign in the territory of its traditional rival, the (then) *Glasgow Herald*, which was clearly fighting back – the small advertisement on the dash ('Scotland's Greatest Newspaper') makes a big claim!

On the same rush-hour duty Standard 338 passes Govan Cross. The lines on the right led into the Govan goods (and former passenger) station, and were used by freight trains to Fairfield shipyard. Behind the tram are the workshops of the Govan shipyard of Harland & Wolff; the yard, workshops and adjacent tenements have now all been replaced by low-density housing.

Preliminary work on the first modern Clyde tunnel had already begun in 1958, as 731 waits at Linthouse on a peak-hour working of service 12.

Right Between Govan and Paisley Road Toll, the trams ran past a dry dock, then around Princes Dock, and the top-deck passengers had a very good view of Glasgow's busy shipping. In the distance to the left of tram 409 are the signals that controlled the movement of ships into and out of the docks, while an Ellerman 'City' liner can be glimpsed next to the Western SMT bus. Car 409 was one of the Standards rebuilt in the post-war years. The overhead for the replacement trolleybuses is already in position in October 1958.

Below Paisley Road West ran for many miles as a wide straight thoroughfare, ideally suited for trams, and apart from an absence of sufficient loading islands it was an impressive demonstration of the capabilities of the modern tramway. On 4 June 1958 Cunarder 1347 is outward bound on service 32 at the junction with the tracks of the 7 at Jura Street; the trees of Bellahouston Park, site of the 1938 Empire Exhibition, are on the right.

On King George V Bridge a cyclist carefully uses the smooth stone tracks laid to assist horses pulling heavy carts over the granite setts. On the parallel railway bridge can be seen one of the many gantries of semaphore signals that controlled the approach to Glasgow Central. Cunarder 1347 is on service 22 on 8 November 1958, and is followed by a GCT Leyland PD2 with Weymann bodywork.

The tenements of Garscube Road in the inner northern suburbs form a backdrop to Standard 217 working service 4 in May 1958. It is followed by one of the city's Education Department grey school buses and a rebodied GCT Daimler. A two-tone Austin Cambridge is parked on the left, while the car parked on the right (a Riley?) was already a vintage model in 1958!

Left Further north, at Saracen Cross, Standard 620 is en route to Springburn on 13 March 1958. The corner of the tenement block has the very common combination of a bank – in this case the Royal Bank of Scotland – and above it a dental surgery; in 1958 banks had neither logos nor cash dispensers. The row of men in cloth caps watching the world go by was a typical scene on many street corners.

Below Car 56, on service 31, and 225, on service 22, stand at Lambhill terminus. This area had, unusually for Glasgow, low-density terrace housing of a basically English style, though built in stone. The conductor of 56 has his hand on the trolley rope ready to pull over the collector as the tram moves off.

Operation of the services in Paisley and Renfrew came to an end on the night of 11 May 1957, and they were replaced the next day by buses of the Scottish Bus Group. On that sad occasion Cunarder 1365, working the last duty on service 4, and Coronation 1277, on the last 28, were photographed at Paisley North. *A. K. Terry*

The 'Yellow Trem': Services 5 and 24

These services had a distinctly middle-class tone, since they ran from one fairly affluent suburb, Clarkston, to another, Kelvinside, whose inhabitants were alleged to refer to the vehicle as a 'trem'. En route the trams also served two important suburban shopping centres, Victoria Road in the south and Byres Road in Hillhead to the west. These ensured good patronage even outside the peak hours.

Left In Battlefield Road there was a short section of reserved track, laid in sett paving rather than ballast. Here Coronation 1221 heads for the terminus at Holmlea Road in June 1956 and a crew member alights to go on duty at the nearby Langside depot.

Below City-bound trams ran along the shopping centre of Victoria Road, then, at Coplaw Street, crossed the single track that was used for driver training in the school car. Cunarder 1333 is outward bound in March 1958; behind it is the Plaza ballroom, well known to generations of young Glaswegians, while, at Eglinton Toll, a steam-hauled train passes under the roadway.

When the tram was king of the road! The traffic of Dumbarton Road has stopped to allow one passenger to alight from car 220 at the Western Infirmary gate in March 1958; at the gate is a cream-painted telephone kiosk. The rather elegant vehicle on the right apparently belongs to the whisky producer Johnnie Walker, though its exact purpose is not clear. The spire of Glasgow University rises in the fog above the roof of the tram.

In the last week of service 24, Standard 297 pauses to pick up passengers at the junction of Church Street and Dumbarton Road. For a Wednesday morning there is very little other traffic about. The tenement block on the right has since been demolished to make way for new buildings for the Western Infirmary, but that on the left and the church beside it remain today; the sandstone has been cleaned and the buildings look much better for it.

Standard 139 swings out of Highburgh Road into Byres Road in 1956. The surrounding buildings have not changed much since then, but the end of the tenement block on the right was, together with a portion of the road behind (Ashton Road), demolished to make way for a car park in the early 1970s. *W. J. Guthrie*

Above The tenements of Clarence Drive are still as handsome today as they were when Standard 481 was on service 24 in July 1956.

Right There was little traffic around at Broomhill Cross when this photograph was taken in March 1958, although a Standard Vanguard can be seen to the left of car 133 on its way to Anniesland. The lack of traffic does allow appreciation of the fine proportions of the 'Scottish Baronial' tenements of 1902 in Broomhill Drive.

Outposts of Empire

Mainly because of the expansionist policies of the first two managers of the municipal system, John Young and James Dalrymple, and the acquisition by the latter of the hitherto independent systems of Airdrie and Coatbridge and Paisley, Glasgow possessed some very long routes, with termini deep in the surrounding counties and, in some cases, deep in the countryside. Most of these services were trimmed to terminate at the city boundary in 1956-57, but some survived until final closure – in fact Glasgow's last tram actually ran in Clydebank!

At the terminus at Airdrie on 2 November 1956, Coronation car 1183 is on service 15. This terminus was of fairly recent origin; until 1953 trams had run on a further 200 yards to the original terminus, but as this involved crossing the busy A73 trunk road, operation was cut back to the west side of that road. The entire service ceased on 3 November 1956. On the hoardings are apparently timeless advertisements for Polo Mints and Wall's Ice Cream.

In August 1955 Kilmarnock Bogie 1105 revisited the haunts of its youth on an enthusiasts' tour to Paisley and Airdrie. Here it stands on the crossover outside Elderslie depot; the line had formerly gone on from here to Kilbarchan, but it was found that the long-wheelbase trucks of the modernised cars would not negotiate the loops in the single track and that section was closed and replaced by GCT buses in 1932.

On the east side of the city, Cambuslang, sometimes reputed to be the largest village in Scotland, was at one time served by the trams of two systems, the Lanarkshire Tramways Company and Glasgow Corporation. The former operator converted to buses in 1931, but the Glasgow trams soldiered on until 3 November 1956. In the summer of that year Standard 322 passes Cambuslang station.

Above Glenfield terminus lay just beyond the built-up area of Paisley and was served by the 28 from Renfrew Ferry. Until 1949 this had been the start of the single-track section through the open country to Barrhead, but in that year the link was cut and the service became purely local and very profitable. Here, 1272, one of Elderslie's Coronations, is about to reverse in April 1957. The 28 closed on 11 May of the same year.

Left It is hard to believe, from this view, that Broomhouse terminus lay on the main A74 road to London. The long twilight of a July evening shows Standard 381 about to set off for Maryhill – not another vehicle is in sight and there appear to be no passengers, the only sign of life being the shadow of the photographer. The service had been cut back to this unlikely terminus from Uddingston town centre in 1948, thus losing much local traffic. The only two places of interest at Broomhouse were a crematorium and the new Calderpark Zoo, but most of the patrons of the former arrived by private transport and British Railways opened a station to serve the latter, leaving even less traffic for the trams. Today the area is covered by a motorway junction and is somewhat busier!

'Red Clydeside': Services 9 and 26

The origin of these services, which came to typify the city's trams as no others did, can be traced back to horse-tram days when there was a 'red' service along Argyle Street. In later years they were operated as 9 and 26 and for a time there was also a 26A. These services lasted until 1962, and the 9 became Glasgow's last service. The route lay almost entirely in industrial areas, with tenement housing, and there was heavy works traffic in both directions, requiring many short workings and special cars. The combined frequency ensured that, west of Bridgeton Cross, there was 'always a car in sight'.

Right The 9 and 26 came to be the home of the Kilmarnock Bogies, as the routes had few curves of any sharpness – indeed, the former had only two in its entire length of 11.73 miles! Here two of these trams, 1127 and 1119, lay over at the terminus at Dalmuir West in August 1960, with one of the Corporation's attractive Daimler single-deck buses on learner duties. The views of the open country of the Kilpatrick Hills reminded older passengers that at one time one could travel on from here by tram to Loch Lomond at Balloch.

Below In Dalmuir there were still in 1962 many signs of the blitz of March 1941. Some of the bombed tenements had been replaced by pre-fab houses of the type seen beyond the advertisement for Aitken's Beers as Coronation 1263 speeds towards the terminus, the blind already set for the return journey. The tram is clearly giving the driver of the Ford Zephyr a good run for his money!

Above Peak-hour traffic at Kelso Street, Yoker, on a wet evening in April 1961: two cyclists, clad in oilskin capes, appear to be trying to find a way around tram 1091 and a GCT AEC bus on service 11A, while a boy in wellingtons plays in the gutter. Beyond the tram pedestrians make for the ferry to Renfrew. The Anchorage Bar is still there today, although it has lost its attractive frosted glass windows, but the National Commercial Bank beyond the tram (then a very recent merger of the National and Commercial Banks) was later, ironically, replaced by a betting shop.

Left There were short workings in both directions on the 9 and 26, and here car 76 is about to reverse at Victoria Park Drive, Scotstoun, to work back out from the city, while a Central SMT Leyland PD2 speeds past on its way inwards. The handsome red sandstone parish church behind the tram, after becoming decrepit and vandalised, has now been demolished and replaced by a block of flats.

Partick is still a busy transport interchange, but the station has been re-located from the left of the picture to the right, to afford easy interchange with the modernised Subway and the new bus station. The former entrance has become a small garden centre, an establishment not known in Partick in 1960, when this photograph was taken. Car 1125 is being (somewhat dangerously) overtaken by a GCT AEC Regent bus, while a Central SMT Leyland appears to be about to follow suit. The Rosevale Cinema, which is situated behind the photographer, is showing *A Terrible Beauty*, a film about the IRA that would not be untopical today; it starred Robert Mitchum and was made in 1960. Later in the week patrons could enjoy *Bottoms Up* (starring Jimmy Edwards and based on the Muir/Norden TV series *Whacko!*) and *Rawhide Trail*, the latter being by then definitely not new! The cinema is now a cut-price supermarket.

Above Little has changed since August 1960 at the bridge over the Kelvin, though today the street lamps have been changed and the Art Galleries, having already been cleaned externally, are now closed for modernisation. The Kelvin Hall, on the left, still houses the Museum of Transport, but this will move to new premises within the next two years. A Kilmarnock Bogie shares the road with two of Glasgow's AEC Regents of 1950.

Below There were not many loading islands on the Glasgow system, but one was to be found at the Argyle Street/Sauchiehall Street junction, where car 1107 pauses to take a passenger in August 1960. The tobacconist's shop is advertising no fewer than three varieties of cigarette – Capstan, Senior Service and Player's – as well as Saint Bruno tobacco. Glaswegians were heavy smokers! Today the stonework of the tenement has been cleaned and the shop has been replaced by a bar called 'The Horse and Tram'.

At Anderston Cross in March 1959, Standard 702 – by then the oldest car in the fleet and all of 60 years of age – heads west on a short working to Scotstoun. There is still an Anderston station, signposted to the left of the tram, but the building carrying the sign has been razed, as have all the surrounding tenements. Today the urban landscape would not encourage the social groups gathered on the left for a 'crack' (chat), and underground toilets and police boxes have alike gone from the scene.

The shops on the left have been redeveloped, and those on the right have been replaced by the Radison Hotel. These developments have considerably changed the character of the western approach to Central station along Argyle Street. Car 1093 appears to be racing a scooter in August 1960.

Above One of the two curves mentioned in the introduction above was at Greendyke Street, where car 1110 is seen heading westwards in November 1960. A timeless Volkswagen 'Beetle' tries to overtake following the Wolseley 4/44, while a Vauxhall Victor pokes out from the left and outside the Oxford Tavern on the right is a classic Humber, complete with rear wheel spats.

Below The 26 and, for some years, the 26A served the fiercely independent burgh of Rutherglen. On 15 April 1961 at Rutherglen Cross, Coronation 1190 is outward-bound and carrying an advertisement ('They Gave Me A Year to Live') with an oddly prophetic warning!

Above Also at Rutherglen Cross on 15 April 1961, looking in other direction towards Burnside, a Kilmarnock Bogie is followed by a Central SMT Leyland, while a Cunarder attacks the climb up Stonelaw Road.

Below Coronation 1154 is followed by a Cunarder on the approach to the Burnside terminus, which was situated in Duke's Road. The Singer Gazelle on the right is almost hidden beneath numerous badges – perhaps its owner entered it in rallies – while a more modest Ford is parked on the other side. The British Linen Bank, on the corner, became a branch of the Bank of Scotland when the two merged in 1971.

This is the terminal crossover in Duke's Road in April 1961. A 'message' (errand) boy carefully pilots his bicycle across the tram lines, while a large coach-built pram is parked outside the Co-op. The Coronation is on service 18, while the Cunarder is on the 26.

Above Auchenshuggle was probably the best known of all Glasgow termini, although it was hardly distinguished for its traffic potential, being situated in an area devoid of housing and just too far from the steelworks to have any works traffic. On a sunny afternoon in April 1961 Standard 76 is about to leave while the crew of Coronation 1264 take a break from service.

Left Shawfield was one of the termini of later years that also served no very obvious traffic need and was chosen either for political reasons or, as in this case, to avoid parallel working of trams and trolleybuses. Greyhound races at the stadium behind car 1190 provided a certain amount of evening traffic, but usually, as on the misty morning of 12 November 1958, there were no passengers.

The 'Yellow Peril'

Service 7 was a relative newcomer to the system, the connecting link across Glasgow Green from Bridgeton to the south side having been opened only in the 1920s. It did not enter the city centre and its main function was to cater for works traffic – at rush hours trams operated to Linthouse, as well as Bellahouston, the normal terminus, and there were heavy loadings in both directions.

Above The Millerston terminus was shared with service 8, on which Coronation 1241 is working in June 1958. Overhead wiring for the trolleybuses that would soon take over the 7 is already in place.

Right Cunarder 1369 picks up some Sunday passengers at a stop in Cumbernauld Road; again it can be seen that the wiring for the trolleybuses is already in place.

Above This stretch of track was used only by the 7 in passenger service, but it also served as a short cut from Dennistoun depot to Alexandra Parade for cars running into service on the 6, so it continued in use after the conversion. Car 657 is taking up an evening peak-hour duty on the latter, and pursues one of the new trolleybuses on 13 March 1959. Usher's beer and Chivers' Olde English Marmalade are advertised on the hoardings.

Left The complicated five-way junction at Bridgeton Cross was one of two on the system to require a signal cabin, the basic square tower to the left of tram 1371. The tram is following a 'mobile shop' and a Central SMT Leyland double-decker and is about to turn right into James Street. The advertisement on the side panel invites *Daily Express* readers to win a country cottage or £4,000, but those who wanted to relax in the summer sun seem quite content to sit under the well-known 'umbrella' on the left!

Above The link across the Clyde was by King's Bridge and through Glasgow Green, where Standard 156 is seen in June 1958.

Right Standard 176 turns from Govan Road into Golspie Street on 4 June 1958. The tenement on the corner houses the premises of the paints department of the South Side Co-operative Society, whose unassuming window display would be lost in today's world of competitive marketing! Above it is the traditional dental surgery, and above the roof of the tram are the cranes of the Fairfield shipyard, one of the two still operating (under different management) on the Upper Clyde.

In 1938 the service was extended by a few hundred yards to connect with Paisley Road West by a triangular junction and provide a service to the Empire Exhibition held in Bellahouston Park. In this view Standard 81 and Cunarder 1380 stand at the terminus in front of a very handsome block of tenements.

The University tram

In post-war days the University terminus was served by the 3 and 14 and the combined frequency was impressive, especially in the morning rush to get to classes starting at 9am. At the terminus obliging drivers would open the front doors on the modern cars and students would stream off at both ends, right into the middle of such traffic as there was. But the trams were diverted away from the terminus in January 1959, to allow repairs to the bridge in Gibson Street, and they did not return.

After the morning rush, Standard 520 takes a breather outside the men's Union building in the summer of 1958. Few students had cars then and most relied on the trams or the Subway to get them to and from classes; however, one car is parked outside the entrance to the Union, and further along a Ford stands ahead of some motorcycles. In the block at the corner of Gibson Street can be seen the white-painted bookshop of A. Stenhouse & Co, suppliers of textbooks to generations of students, and, beyond, the white sun-blinds of Greengates tea-room.

After service 3 was diverted to Park Road, cars had to take a layover between those passing on service 10. Coronation 1394 of 1954 stands outside the shop of J. G. Murray, tailor, while 1372 passes on the 10 and Lansdowne church looms behind. On 1394 the poster for the *Daily Express* offers prizes of £500 or a car worth £1,000, while the *Evening Citizen*, as advertised on 1372, is more concerned with social affairs, in this case 'Divorce'.

Service 23

The 23 was another fairly new service, having been introduced only in 1943. Over the years the route was changed several times, and as late as 1957 it was extended from Gairbraid Avenue to Maryhill, the last service extension in Glasgow. It was finally replaced by buses on 7 November 1960.

Left At the original terminus at Airdrie in March 1952, a Standard car works the 23, a Coronation is on the 15 and there are some old houses to the left. Very shortly afterwards Standards ceased to work on the 23, which became an all-Coronation service.

Below left The local service between Airdrie and Coatbridge was neither one thing nor the other! It operated, under what could be called a flying fraction, as the 15/23. In the twilight of a November afternoon, a Standard has just come out of the local depot to take up service.

Above right The 23 traversed the town centres of Airdrie and Coatbridge before reaching, at Langloan, the fine reserved track built by Glasgow between 1923 and 1925, to link the formerly separate local system with its own tracks at Baillieston. In July 1956 Coronation 1235 (on the 15) enters this track.

Right The service was curtailed to Baillieston in October 1954, and in 1957 the terminus was relocated at Martin Crescent to avoid a crossing of the ever busier A8. Coronation 1245 is seen there on 4 November 1960.

Above By August 1960 the setts in the carriageway in Duke Street have been replaced by asphalt, but they remain between the rails, a form of surfacing quite common in the later years. Beyond the tenements on the right were the low buildings of Glasgow's former cattle market at Bellgrove. By this date private cars were increasing in number, even in tenement districts, and here these include a Standard 10 on the left and a Renault Dauphine on the right.

Below George Square was the centrepiece of the late-18th-century new town of Glasgow and has an area of 2 acres. In November 1960 car 1206 heads west at Queen Street. The buildings to the left of the bus, the last remnant of the original development, have since been torn down and replaced by yet another office block, while the North British Hotel has passed out of railway control and has been modernised as the Copthorne. Even on a cold November morning, little boys wore short trousers!

Above On the same day, Albert, Prince Consort, appears to be riding across the roof of the modern tourist office on the left, while car 1288 loads at George Square for Baillieston. This building has fortunately since been removed.

Below Cars terminating in the city centre used the crossover at the end of the track in St Vincent Street, where 1208 sits astride the crossover in August 1960. The driver seems to have abandoned the tram to admire the fine Humber parked at the kerb! Crossing the street in the background is a Triumph Herald coupé.

On 11 March 1960 car 1259 is about to turn right in Cambridge Street, on a section of track relaid in asphalt in 1957. Today the view from the same spot is unrecognisable, and none of the original buildings survive.

Fords were clearly popular in Maryhill in August 1960. Prototype Coronation 1141 is flanked by two Consuls at Bilsland Drive, while a Ford van and another Consul follow. The Jowett Javelin parked on the left affords some variety!

THE CARS

There were several North American terms used on the Glasgow system – the orange colour was officially 'cadmium yellow' and the running number, held in a metal stencil in the front offside window of the lower saloon, was the 'route number' (normally pronounced 'rout'). But above all the trams themselves were always 'cars' or 'caurs' to both staff and passengers alike. This section shows the various types that were in use after 1945.

The Standards

Next to the E/E1 Class of trams of the London County Council, the most numerous class of tram to run in Britain was the Glasgow Standard, first introduced in 1898 and destined to remain in operation until the summer of 1961. Eventually 1,005 were built, and after 1923 the 20 newest Paisley cars were rebuilt to a very similar design. Of course the first two examples of 1898 had little in common with the final survivors, for the Standards, like the American PCC car, had the great merit of having a sound basic design on to which later modifications could be grafted without extensive alteration to the basic frame. In their final totally enclosed condition, with air brakes, two 60hp motors and upholstered seats on both decks, the Standards were fast and comfortable vehicles and, until the decline set in after 1956, could hold their own with any contemporary bus.

The general anatomy of the Standard can be seen in this view of 942 awaiting home-going workers in the siding in Porterfield Road, Renfrew, in April 1957. It is from the earliest batch and has a round dash; ventilation to the lower saloon is by a monitor strip and clerestory. The platforms are roomy and afford plenty of space for the conductor to stand apart from the flow of passengers. The platform at the driver's end could be used for the carriage of luggage, prams, boxes of flowers or other articles, and it is said that some people accomplished a complete 'flitting' (house removal) by tram.

Above Seen at the University terminus in April 1957 is 438; one of the first Glasgow trams to have a covered top deck (in 1904), it also has glass ventilators to the lower saloon. The University Union, seen behind the tram, was then strictly for men students only; lady students, as they were officially known, were allowed in only when dances were being held!

Below The basic design was developed into the 'hex dash' pattern from 1910 onwards. These cars were built with vestibuled platforms, earlier cars being later retro-fitted with this refinement. All Standard trams were modernised between 1928 and 1931, to receive enclosed upper decks, upholstered seating, air brakes and newer and more powerful motors; bow collectors replaced the trolley poles shortly afterwards. Here, fresh from overhaul in September 1955, 39 is being shunted by the motor school car and paintshop shunter, 1017. *A. K. Terry*

The end of a Standard – 237 is broken up in Coplawhill Works, its birthplace, in May 1959.

The upper saloon of 176. Seats were covered in brown or blue leather and the woodwork was stained black, although some cars had this repainted white in the 1950s, in an effort to impart a brighter appearance.

The Green Goddesses

These trams seemed to be an excellent bargain when Glasgow acquired its first batch of 25 in 1953. They were fast – a letter in the *Evening Times* claimed that one had been timed at 48mph on the open road between Maryhill and Killermont – smooth riding and comfortable, if lacking the Art Deco elegance of the Coronations. Encouraged by their reception by the public, Glasgow bought a further 22 in 1954, but even as they arrived, troubles began. Years of neglect in Liverpool had taken their toll. Lack of bulkheads in the lower deck led to drooping platforms, and it was found that rainwater very easily made its way into the driving position. There were also constant problems with the electric wiring, which in the end had to be totally renewed. The high-backed seats, comfortable for the passengers, were inclined to catch the conductors' 'Ultimate' ticket machines and were finally replaced by seats from scrapped Standard cars. In the event the Standards outlived the Goddesses and the last of the latter was scrapped at Coplawhill in July 1960.

The first Goddess to be put into service was 1006, in October 1953.
Six months later it is seen at Tollcross, still very recognisably a Liverpool tram.

Above Another member of the same batch, 1023, picks up a good load at Glasgow Cross in June 1959. By now the cars had acquired small opening windows at the ends of the upper saloon, to allow access to the bow rope. Behind the tram is one of Bayne & Duckett's shoe shops, of which there were many in the city. They had disappeared by the mid-1970s, but Younger's beer, as advertised on the distant gable, is, of course, still very much a part of the Glasgow scene. This view shows the Maley & Taunton swing-link trucks fitted to this class of tram, a design that gave a particularly smooth ride.

Below In a wintry scene at Tollcross early in 1959, we see car 1049, one of the second batch and fitted with EMB lightweight trucks, of the same design as used on the Glasgow Coronations.

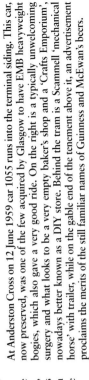

At Anderston Cross on 12 June 1959 car 1055 runs into the terminal siding. This car, now preserved, was one of the few acquired by Glasgow to have EMB heavyweight bogies, which also gave a very good ride. On the right is a typically unwelcoming surgery and what looks to be a very empty baker's shop and a 'Crafts Emporium'; nowadays better known as a DIY store. Behind the tram is a Scammell 'mechanical horse' with trailer, while on the gable end of the tenement above it, an advertisement proclaims the merits of the still familiar names of Guinness and McEwan's beers.

Car 1030 is seen among the traffic in Argyle Street in June 1959. The attractive but impractical curved end windows had been replaced on many cars by flat glass, in an effort to cure the problem of leaking rainwater. Fascination with royalty was as strong in 1959 as it is today, and the *Evening Times* was running a series on 'The Queen at Home'. To the left, Littlewood's store is under construction, while beside the van is an Austin A35 followed by two Bedford vans.

Left The twilight of a Goddess: car 1029 is broken up in Coplawhill Works in May 1959.

The Kilmarnock Bogies

These were the most 'English' trams ever to run in Scotland, being based on the E1 Class of the London County Council. Intended for the service from Paisley to Airdrie, they had disgraced themselves by a distressing tendency to derail on curves in the city centre and were soon transferred to the services along Dumbarton Road and Argyle Street, on which there were almost no curves and where their high capacity proved to be very useful. During the war the lower saloon seats on all but one of the class were altered to a longitudinal pattern to accommodate more standing passengers, and they remained thus so that passengers could contemplate each other carefully as the car rolled its way westwards from the city.

Below On a short working of service 26, 1119 stands in the terminal siding at Scotstoun in March 1959. The maximum traction trucks, built by the Kilmarnock Engineering Company, can clearly be seen.

The Coronations

First introduced in December 1936, these cars were considered by many to be Glasgow's finest. Fast and smooth-riding, they provided for passengers and crew a luxury not before (and often not recently) known in urban transport. The entrance was especially well designed, with two steps giving access to a roomy platform from which one small step led into the lower saloon. The seats, brown 'jazz' moquette downstairs, green leather with red trim upstairs, were really comfortable, and passengers even had the amenity of an armrest under the window.

However, there were drawbacks. For the expense and complication of four motors, the seating capacity of 64 was very low, and the cost of running these cars was one of the factors that led to the experiments with modern four-wheel cars in 1940. The elaborate Art Deco 'Alhambrinal' ceiling panels became dirty and discoloured (especially upstairs) and in some cars were replaced with white laminate in the 1950s. The very attractive lamp covers shed a warm light on wet nights, but they did tend to work loose and could make a considerable din when the car reached any speed. But perhaps the worst feature was the absence of opening windows and reliance on ventilation by fans, which were supposed to, but often did not, feed fresh air into the saloons; in practice there was almost always a good 'fug' on the upper deck, and on Glasgow's hot days – of which there were many in years such as 1949 and 1955 – both saloons became intolerable and the only solution was to open doors and end windows and rely on a gale to keep passengers and crew cool.

In basically original condition, car 1242 stands at Anniesland Cross terminus on service 24 in July 1956.

Above The Coronations received several modifications after 1949. The two-piece windscreen was replaced by a single pane, the air intake above it was panelled over, and the opening window at the end of the upper saloon was modified to give quicker access to the rope for the bow collector. In this condition an unidentified car turns from St Vincent Street into Hope Street in August 1960; unusually no service number is shown. The pedestrian in the white coat seems to be oblivious of the tram's approach, apparently to the interest of all the passengers!

Below A man in a cloth cap fumbles for his fare on the upper deck of a Coronation. The decor, though somewhat grubby, is basically the original – the lampshades were striped green and white and the inadequate, and by now thoroughly dirty, ventilators can be seen. The poster behind the passenger was part of an anti-litter campaign, though litter was not then the problem it has since become, while that on the right advertises evening classes. Below the end window can just be seen the cabinet that contained the destination blinds. There was no need to hang upside down out of the window to change these!

Above The second experimental car, 1142, could be distinguished by the five side windows in the saloon. Its Maley & Taunton trucks gave a very comfortable ride, but despite this it was latterly confined to peak-hour workings on service 25. It was a favourite for enthusiasts' tours and is seen here on one of these, at Pollokshaws West: this terminus was not used in regular service. *W. J. Guthrie*

Below The interior of 1142. *W. J. Guthrie collection*

In 1954 six more Coronations were built, using trucks that had been obtained from Liverpool. They were slightly simpler, and perhaps slightly neater in design, the most obvious difference being the plain panels above the lower-deck windows. Car 1398 was the last tram to be built for Glasgow, and is seen here at Merrylee in November 1959.

The Cunarders

Following the experimental 1005, 100 modern trams were turned out by Coplawhill Works between 1948 and 1952. Officially designated Mark II Coronations, they were soon dubbed Cunarders and the name stuck. The chance was taken to remedy the few design faults on the pre-war trams, so ventilation was much improved, the lighting was concealed behind a fixed panel and there were more seats.

Unfortunately the excellent doorway layout was changed to one with a three-step entrance and a thick central pillar, which made it impossible to take a pram aboard, and the doorway was a nightmare to anyone with impaired mobility. As befitted their name, the Cunarders tended to roll, rather alarmingly at first, then, when the suspension had been altered, with a pleasant swaying motion. They were handsome and comfortable cars and deserved a longer career than they had.

At Mosspark terminus in May 1952, 1336 shows the second style of painting applied to the class, with the downswept green band dividing the two indicator boxes.

The awkward layout of the doorway can be seen on 1347, at the Springburn terminus of service 27 on 12 March 1958. The age of the jet airliner had not yet arrived, and the turbo-prop was still something of a novelty, of which British European Airways were more than a little proud!

Odd men out

As the Glasgow fleet was so highly standardised, there was not the variety of tram types to be found in some other cities, but the few non-standard cars were always of interest to the enthusiast – passengers probably did not notice the difference!

Below One of the most comfortable cars in the fleet was single-decker 1089, the tram that refused to die! Originally built as an experimental high-speed car, with a separate entrance and exit, it was converted to normal layout in 1932 and put to work on the only service that used single-deckers, the 20 from Clydebank to Duntocher.

It was out on the road on one of the nights of the Clydebank blitz, but, although trapped for some time at the upper end of the line until it could be removed by lorry, it escaped serious damage. When the line closed in December 1949, 1089 was stored for two years, then re-entered service on shipyard specials with many of its seats removed to allow maximum standing capacity. Alterations of the rules about standing passengers once again threatened the car, but it emerged from store after the Dalmarnock fire, and thus survived for ultimate preservation. It is seen here at Yoker on a wet evening in April 1961, the white-coated policeman on point duty having stood aside to let it, and the following queue of trams, pass towards Clydebank.

Below In this second view 1089 has just come out of Partick depot and is flanked by what must have been a fairly new Mini (left) and an equally new Ford Anglia (right), while a blue 'invalid tricycle' heads down Hayburn Street and a Central SMT Leyland PD2 passes on Dumbarton Road in the distance. *W. J. Guthrie*

The single-ended double-decker 1005 of 1947 was Glasgow's most original tram. In its first colour scheme of dark blue, kingfisher blue and sky blue, it was a beautiful vehicle and brightened the austerity years of the late 1940s. It was especially noticeable at night when the fluorescent lighting drew much attention, and even some complaints! It was first operated on the only circular service, the 33. In later years the operators did not seem to know what to do with it and, shorn of many of its experimental features and repainted in the standard colours, it migrated to special working between Maryhill depot and the Moir Street loop at Glasgow Cross, where these pictures were taken in July 1953.

Below Finally, in 1956 1005 was converted to double-ended condition, the last tram to be rebuilt by Glasgow. It still had the peculiarity that the two ends were dissimilar; the original front end seen here was quite unlike the Cunarder style of the former rear end! This view was taken at Tollcross in 1957. *W. J. Guthrie*

Below The experimental four-wheel cars of 1940 were a mixed bunch, no two being quite identical. While some re-used old equipment, others, such as 1002, seen here at Renfrew Ferry in June 1953, were entirely new. This tram rode very smoothly on a Maley & Taunton truck. The entrance was particularly well-designed, with only two steps from street level, the lower being only 234mm (about 9 inches) above the ground when the car was loaded; few present-day 'low floor' trams have achieved such a figure. Unfortunately the cars entered service in wartime and, with their non-standard features, caused additional problems for the hard-pressed maintenance staff; the result was that nobody really loved them. In 1951, the four, plus nominal rebuild 6, were exiled to Elderslie depot, but even there they were used only on peak-hour workings. When the Paisley routes closed, they had a brief sojourn at Govan depot, before being scrapped in 1959. Only 1003 ever carried large advertisement panels, but 1002 sports a small 'See You at Butlin's' poster, the holiday camp near Ayr being a favourite of Glaswegians in the 1950s.

It is not clear why the GCT engineers decided to rebuild Kilmarnock Bogie 1100 in 1940/41 in the way they did, unless it was to have a mobile test-bed to try out new features for the post-war cars. Externally it was given altered ends, which bore some resemblance to those of the Coronation cars, but it was an unhappy combination of styles and 1100 lacked both the functional simplicity of the Kilmarnocks and the elegance of the Coronations. For once, Glasgow copied a feature of Edinburgh's trams and the car had colour service lights (not visible in this view), which in the event were not used. Internally the car was little altered, but it did receive new stairs and brown leather seats from a Standard car. Despite its gawky appearance, 1100 performed well enough and gave years of service on shipyard specials from Partick depot. It is seen here at Yoker in April 1961, with a Central SMT Leyland PD1 jostling for road space. The service number displayed under the offside cab window was latterly unique to this tram.

When the Paisley system was taken over in 1923, the 20 newest cars, which were nevertheless of a very old-fashioned design, were rebuilt to the then Glasgow standard and in due course were modernised together with the rest of the Standards. They could, however, always be distinguished by the lower-deck windows, which were of the LCC pattern. In this view at Elderslie depot, 1068 poses in the yard after withdrawal. It is now preserved at Crich, restored to open-top condition and Paisley District livery. *W. J. Guthrie*

Off the normal beat

While the Standard cars were to be seen all over the city, other types were to be found only on certain services, while diversions could sometimes bring trams on to stretches of track not normally used for passenger service.

Cunarder trams did not normally work along St Vincent Place, and 1311, on an un-numbered special working to Partick on Sunday 17 May 1959, is seen turning into Renfield Street. Pedestrian 'Cross Now' signals had just been installed at this busy junction; these have now been replaced by today's more familiar pictograms.

The Kilmarnock Bogies were not often found away from their usual haunts of Argyle Street/Dumbarton Road. Returning from the Car Works, 1117 follows a Coronation up Union Street; it will loop round via St Vincent Street and Hope Street to rejoin Argyle Street. The entrance to Central station has now lost its attractive canopy (on the extreme left) and the Canadian Fur Co next door would probably not find much business in today's altered fashion climate.

After 1951 the experimental four-wheel streamliners were seldom seen in the city centre. In this view in Renfield Street, taken hurriedly on the morning of 26 February 1959, car 6 was probably on its last journey to the scrapyard. The News Theatre and cafeteria seen on the left were one of the innovations of the 1950s, but were later overtaken by television.

Above Coronation trams were not used on service 7, due to clearance problems in Golspie Street, Govan, and this view of 1270 at the junction of Crown and Ballater Streets is therefore unusual. This was a workmen's special to Linthouse. *W. J. Guthrie*

Right The single track in Greenview Street was used only for depot workings. In this view, Cunarder 1333, on a special tour, pauses outside Pollokshaws Town Hall. *W. J. Guthrie*

It was often alleged by their detractors that trams were 'inflexible', but the complexity of Glasgow's track layout allowed some scope for diversions when necessary. On 12 March 1958 there was a problem in Victoria Road and southbound cars on service 24 were diverted to run via the line in Coplaw Street, normally used only for training purposes. Here car 1298 prepares to turn off Pollokshaws Road; as the points at this junction were normally set for the main line, the motorman has had to leave his cab to change them by hand.

Depots

There were in modern times 11 depots, ranging from tiny Coatbridge to Newlands, which held over 200 cars. Most were situated in areas of tenement housing, allowing staff to live near their work and go home between 'split' shifts.

Above Elderslie was the main depot of the former Paisley system, but with a capacity of only 47 cars, it was small compared to those elsewhere in Glasgow and retained something of the atmosphere of a family business until the end, which came on 11 May 1957. It lay several hundred yards beyond the terminus of the same name and had a distinctly rural aspect. In this view, taken in May 1952, car 6 occupies the end road of an otherwise empty shed.

Right Partick depot was an almost total contrast, large (124 cars) and situated in the heart of the industrial city, providing many extra cars for shipyard and factory specials along Dumbarton Road. There was an individual entrance to each lye and in this view, taken early in 1961, a Kilmarnock Bogie has come out of one of the further roads, while an apparently abandoned pram stands against the wall.

Newlands was a relatively modern depot, opened in 1926 to replace an ex-horse tram shed nearby. Unlike most of the other depots, it was situated in a leafy and affluent suburb. In 1948 Newlands experienced one of Glasgow's two depot fires of the electric era, but prompt action limited the loss to only a few cars. In June 1959 car 812 emerges into Newlandsfield Road.

Possilpark depot was of a different layout, with a single entrance, from which car 249 peeps shyly in March 1958, while a group of staff have a chat outside.

Special occasions

Right up to the end Glasgow maintained the tradition of running illuminated trams to commemorate special occasions or for propaganda. The latter purpose led to the decoration of a tram to encourage people to be X-rayed in the campaign of 1957, while the former brought works car No 29 to the streets in August 1959 to promote the Scottish Industries Exhibition being held that month in the Kelvin Hall. *W. J. Guthrie*

The ones that got away

As the Glasgow trams lasted well into the era of preservation, it is not surprising that a total of 20 cars that ran in Glasgow have survived complete, one of these being in Paris and one in Maine.

One ex-Liverpool tram was saved thanks to the efforts of a group of Merseyside enthusiasts. On 8 June 1960 tram 1055 is about to start on its journey back to England on a low-loader pulled by a Scammell tractor on which the word 'heavy' seems to be superfluous! As Liverpool 869, this car is now running at the National Tramway Museum at Crich.

Car 585 approaches Elmbank Street in Sauchiehall Street on 4 June 1960. In a moment passers-by would hear a 'clonk' as the automatic points changed to allow the car to turn right. Minis have now become part of the street scene, and yet another motorcycle combination is visible ahead of the parked Ford. On the upper deck a passenger enjoys the view and fresh air at the open window of the end balcony. As can be seen, the bodywork on 585 was somewhat bowed and the car was not originally a candidate for preservation, but the loss of the rather better 526 in the Dalmarnock fire in March 1961 saved it, and it is now, painted with the blue route colour, a static exhibit in the Science Museum in London.

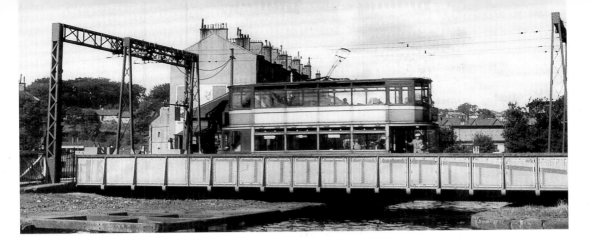

Above The swing bridge on the Forth & Clyde Canal at Dalmuir was closed for repair from September 1959, at first to trams only but from April 1960 to all traffic, and many doubted that trams would ever cross it again. However, the service was re-instated when the bridge re-opened on 1 August 1960. Later that month Kilmarnock Bogie 1115, now preserved at Crich, crosses on its way to Dalmuir West.

Below There were at one time many double-deck trams in service in Paris, but the last ran in 1929, long before preservation was thought of. When in 1960 the French museum group, AMTUIR, began to look around for a suitable double-decker to deputise for their own, there were not many left to choose from! It seemed that the Glasgow Standard bore a passing resemblance to the trams of the Chemins de Fer Nogentais, which had once served the western suburbs of Paris, and accordingly 488 was set aside. Before it could be sent off, however, it was briefly returned to traffic following the Dalmarnock fire, and it is seen here at Yoker on a very wet evening in April 1961. As some cloth-capped passengers board, a Leyland bus on tram replacement service 58 waits behind. 'New Heinz soups in a packet', as in the Heinz advert on the right, are still very much around today, but the tiny washing machine with the hand-cranked mangle featured in the Omo advertisement would itself find a place in a museum, and the Glasgow *Evening Citizen* has disappeared into oblivion. The tram is still in France but has deteriorated somewhat in recent years; as the AMTUIR group is at present homeless, it is not on public display.

A group of passengers move out to board 779 in Union Street on the sunny morning of 29 October 1959. This car was later rebuilt as a 'red' car, took part in the final procession in September 1962, and today can be seen in the Glasgow Museum of Transport in the Kelvin Hall.

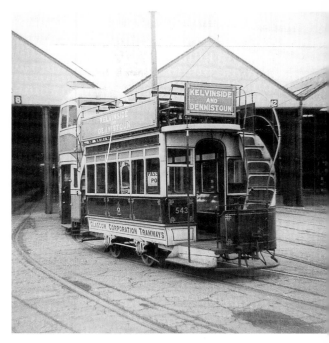

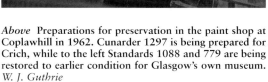

Above Preparations for preservation in the paint shop at Coplawhill in 1962. Cunarder 1297 is being prepared for Crich, while to the left Standards 1088 and 779 are being restored to earlier condition for Glasgow's own museum. *W. J. Guthrie*

Above right The preserved Glasgow horse-car 543, photographed at Newlands depot. *W. J. Guthrie*

Right Motor school car 1017 was a former Paisley car, cut down to single-deck form. It is seen here outside Coplawhill Works in 1959. When it was no longer required, it was purchased privately for preservation and for many years stood in a garden in Cambuslang, bereft of its truck. Now, mounted on an ex-Porto truck, it has been thoroughly restored and in 2004 entered public service at the Summerlee Museum at Coatbridge.

THE PERMANENT WAY

The work of the Permanent Way Department, and its large fleet of associated cars, was always a source of interest to enthusiasts and to those who simply liked to stand and watch the action. Until 1956 Glasgow maintained its track to a high standard and rails were relaid as necessary, corrugations in the track smoothed out and the granite setts carefully packed with tarmacadam. Much of the work had perforce to be done at night, but minor operations could be done by day, with only brief interruption to service.

The junction leading into the terminal spur at Whiteinch, by then no longer in regular service, receives attention on 13 March 1959. A workman with a pneumatic drill (but no ear protectors) is breaking up the setts around the points, while a colleague repacks others. The obligatory barrow is parked nearby and a pedestrian, walking in the carriageway, looks on with interest. Cunarder 1356 on service 26 waits until the workmen stand clear while Standard 257 makes off to Scotstoun on the 6.

Above An essential part of any permanent way operation was the preparation of large quantities of tarmacadam in boilers, which were mounted on two axles and sported a long chimney; they resembled an early locomotive and, when being pulled along a street, made a considerable and probably comparable noise. But the smell of newly boiled tar was pleasant and was said to help recovery from whooping cough, still a common ailment in 1959. Here the western end of Sauchiehall Street is receiving attention and the boilers are on site; with a workmen's hut and several barrels, they have complete occupation of the eastbound carriageway, where they form a marked contrast to the modern motor cars – including a Hillman Minx and a Triumph Mayflower – parked outside the elegant early-19th-century terrace. Car 1198 is on service 14.

Right There was a large fleet of works cars associated with the permanent way gang, but these were shy, nocturnal vehicles, not often photographed. However, in 1958 sand car No 39 ventures out to collect sand from the dryer in Admiral Street, and is seen here passing some track work. Unlike many of the other p.w. cars, this one had been built new, in 1939. *W. J. Guthrie*

By contrast, No 29, a tool van and welding car, had been rebuilt from a passenger car, in this case ex-Paisley 7, latterly Glasgow 1007. It is seen in Coplawhill Works in May 1959, along with another tool van that clearly shows its origins as a Standard car.

The end of the line

The original conversions were regarded as experimental and the tracks abandoned were left in situ for some years.

Only after 1953 was the Corporation sufficiently sure of its actions to take them up. In March 1954 work was under way in Kilbowie Road, Clydebank, to remove the tracks of service 20, which had last run in December 1949.

INDEX OF LOCATIONS